D1622817

take it
personally

*A Practical Guide to Owning and
Obeying the Great Commission*

paul chappell

Copyright © 2016 by Striving Together Publications. All Scripture quotations are taken from the King James Version. Special emphasis in verses is added.

First published in 2016 by Striving Together Publications, a ministry of Lancaster Baptist Church, Lancaster, CA 93535. Striving Together Publications is committed to providing tried, trusted, and proven books that will further equip local churches to carry out the Great Commission. Your comments and suggestions are valued.

All rights reserved. No part of this book may be reproduced, stored in a retrieval system, or transmitted in any form or by any means—electronic, mechanical, photocopy, recording, or otherwise—without written permission of the publisher, except for brief quotations in printed reviews.

Striving Together Publications
4020 E. Lancaster Blvd.
Lancaster, CA 93535
800.201.7748

Cover design by Andrew Jones
Layout by Craig Parker
Writing assistance by Monica Bass

The author and publication team have put forth every effort to give proper credit to quotes and thoughts that are not original with the author. It is not our intent to claim originality with any quote or thought that could not readily be tied to an original source.

ISBN 978-1-59894-324-5

Printed in the United States of America

To Jerry and Bonnie Ferrso—co-laborers in ministry who have compassionately and consistently owned and obeyed the Great Commission.

Thank you for leading our church family to reach our community with the gospel and investing yourselves to train new soulwinners.

Contents

A Note to Pastors, Outreach Directors, and Teachers . . vii

PART ONE: **Making a Difference** 1

  1. The Value of One 5

  2. To Seek and To Save 11

  3. Owning the Mission 17

PART TWO: **Presenting the Gospel** 25

  4. Sharing the Gospel 29

  5. Dealing with Common Questions 45

  6. Making a Soulwinning Visit 57

PART THREE: **Establishing New Christians** . . . 73

  7. Early Instruction 79

  8. Nurturing Growth 91

  9. Committed to Multiplication 97

PART FOUR: **Being an Effective Witness** 105

  10. Using a Prospect List 109

  11. Developing an "Everywhere Mentality" . . . 117

  12. Staying Motivated 127

APPENDIX A: Resources for Outreach and Discipleship . 135

APPENDIX B: Teaching Outlines 139

A Note to Pastors, Outreach Directors, and Teachers

The Great Commission was not given just to pastors. It was given to the local church, and it is a command applicable to every child of God.

Take It Personally is written as a guide for every Christian, and it emphasizes the personal nature of our responsibility to share the gospel of Jesus Christ. It is meant to be an equipping resource for individuals to learn how to share their faith, to lead someone to Christ, and to help a new Christian take early steps of growth in Christ.

As church leaders, however, our job is to equip God's people for this great work. Ephesians 4:11–12 says, "And he gave some, apostles; and some, prophets; and some, evangelists; and some, pastors and teachers; For the perfecting of the saints, *for the work of the ministry,* for the edifying of the body of Christ."

I'd like to suggest three ways that you can involve your church family in the Great Commission.

INVOLVE OTHERS THROUGH TEACHING

Although written for every Christian, *Take It Personally* can also be used as a teaching resource. It is divided into four parts, with each part having three chapters. Thus, you can use this as a four-week teaching tool in a church-wide soulwinning training program. (It could be used in adult Bible classes, small group Bible studies, and other venues as well.)

I recommend using each part as one lesson and each chapter within the part as a main teaching point in the lesson. The headings within each chapter make your sub points. (I've outlined the book for you in this way and have included these teaching lessons in Appendix B.)

A corresponding workbook, with outlines that follow this pattern, is available through Striving Together Publications. In addition to the lesson outlines, it provides the support Scriptures found in this text and can be a helpful tool to put in the hands of those you are teaching.

INVOLVE OTHERS THROUGH ORGANIZED OUTREACH

I believe that my job as a Christian is to share the gospel, and I do on a regular basis. But I believe that my job as a pastor is to equip others to share the gospel.

Thirty years ago, I became the pastor of Lancaster Baptist Church. That very first Sunday evening, I invited the small congregation present to come back to church Tuesday evening for organized outreach. From that first week forward, members of our church have gone out into our community every week sharing the gospel of Christ.

We call it TEAM Soulwinning—Training Every Available Member. Although *Take It Personally* does not explain how to establish and organize a church outreach program, I have written on these topics in detail in the books *Out of Commission* and *Order in the Church* (both available through Striving Together Publications).

Although any Christian should be prepared to share the gospel with anyone anywhere, having organized outreach as a church not only provides specific opportunities for Christians to share their faith, but it shows that a church is taking the Great Commission seriously and is intent on saturating their community with the gospel.

INVOLVE OTHERS THROUGH YOUR EXAMPLE

Soulwinning is one of the many areas of the Christian life that is better caught than taught. You can teach someone how to present the gospel, how to make a church soulwinning visit, and how to explain baptism to a new Christian (and *Take It Personally* is designed to aid you in that instruction), but a soulwinner's *heart* is better caught than taught.

It is as you are faithful in your outreach and as you invite others to join you that they will best learn to share their faith.

There is an old Chinese proverb that says, "Tell me, and I'll forget. Show me, and I'll remember. Involve me, and I'll understand."

I pray that this book will be a help to you as you involve Christians in your church in regularly, passionately, and accurately sharing the gospel of Jesus Christ.

PART ONE

Making a Difference

One day, a man was walking near the ocean shoreline littered with starfish that had been beached on the sand from a recent storm.

As the man walked, he came upon a young boy frantically picking up the dying starfish and throwing them back into the ocean.

"Son," the man smiled as he placed his hand on the boy's shoulder. "You know what you're doing is futile, right?"

The boy didn't reply. He hardly even looked up. He just reached for another starfish and hurled it into the ocean.

The man tried again. "Look," he pointed along the shore. "There are *miles* of washed up starfish. Tens of thousands of them."

The boy grunted as he reached for another.

"You could be here all day and all the next day and the day after that…you could be here all *week*, and you wouldn't make a difference in all these starfish."

For the first time the boy turned to look at the man. He stood as tall as he could with his shoulders back, chin tilted, and starfish in hand. Then he turned and threw the starfish into the ocean. Once again he looked at the man. "Made a difference for that one."

And then he bent down to pick up another.

We long for significance—to make a difference with our lives. And those of us who know the Lord long for others to know Him as well. But sometimes we look at the world around us and wonder if anything we do could actually make a difference.

After all, there are over seven *billion* people in this world. To share the gospel with each of them in groups of one hundred would take four *thousand* years. Even if we could live long enough to do that, they wouldn't all respond. After all, don't we each know people in our own families and circles of acquaintances who aren't interested in being saved?

Yet, as we look in the pages of God's Word, we find that we are commanded—commissioned—to go to others with the gospel. And we find that *every* Christian has this commission.

When you think of it, that's a privilege. Not every Christian is called to be a pastor. Not every Christian is called to be a foreign missionary. Not every Christian is called to a public teaching ministry. But every Christian *is* called to go to others with the gospel—to personally deliver the life-changing gospel of Jesus Christ. And when we take it personally to one person at a time, God uses our witness to make a difference—an *eternal* difference—one life at a time.

So, yes, we can look up and down the shoreline and see hundreds of thousands of starfish; we can look around the world and see billions of people; we can look at our own communities and see vast numbers of people—and we can wonder if we'll ever make a difference.

Or, we can hear Christ's call, rely on the Holy Spirit, and personally share the gospel—and we can make a difference to that *one*. And teach that *one* to do the same. And multiply the *ones* who are reaching that *one*.

In these pages, I invite you to learn how to effectively own and obey the Great Commission of Jesus Christ.

CHAPTER ONE

The Value of One

After the terrorist attacks on September 11, 2001, the former mayor of New York City, Rudy Giuliani, was asked to share a few thoughts:

> "When everybody was fleeing that building, and the cops and the firefighters and the EMS people were heading up into it, do you think any of them said, 'I wonder how many blacks are up there for us to save? I wonder what percentage are whites up here? How many Jews are there? Let's see—are these people making $400,000 a year, or $24,000? No, when you're saving lives, they're all precious... I'm convinced that God wants us to...value every human life the way He does."

Mayor Giuliani was referring to physically saving lives. But his words are true, and they ring just as surely in regard to rescuing people from an eternity apart from God: "…they're all precious…God wants us to…value every human life the way He does."

Indeed, Jesus placed tremendous value on every life.

In His ministry on earth, Christ went out of the way to reach individuals. Even in the parables Christ told, He stressed the value of individuals. In just one chapter, Luke 15, He used stories of a shepherd out searching for *one* lost sheep, a woman searching for *one* lost coin, and a father waiting for his wayward son to tell us how highly God values a single soul. He told us all heaven rejoices when just one sinner is saved: "Likewise, I say unto you, there is joy in the presence of the angels of God over one sinner that repenteth" (Luke 15:10).

Why is one soul so valuable?

A SOUL IS ETERNAL

God created the human soul in His own image (Genesis 1:27). Among other things, this means that we have an eternal soul. Since sin entered the world, our bodies decay and die. But our souls never die.

Most people don't get up every morning and think about eternity. For that matter, most people don't get up every morning and think about the fact that they will one day die. Satan actively works to distract us with the here and now.

In reality, however, when you compare the length of our life on earth to the length of eternity, it looks like this:

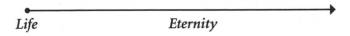

Life　　　　　　　　　　*Eternity*

Even the best life on earth that ends without Christ will bring the worst eternity. This is why Jesus pointed out, "For what shall it profit a man, if he shall gain the whole world, and lose his own soul?" (Mark 8:36).

This is why you and I must remember that every person has an eternal soul.

HEAVEN AND HELL ARE REAL

Not only does every person's soul live somewhere forever, but the Bible is clear that there are only two places where that can be: Heaven or Hell.

Jesus spoke often of both. In fact, He spoke more often of Hell than of Heaven. He even gave us a glimpse into two men's experience in eternity:

> *And it came to pass, that the beggar died, and was carried by the angels into Abraham's bosom: the rich man also died, and was buried; And in hell he lift up his eyes, being in torments, and seeth Abraham afar off, and Lazarus in his bosom. And he cried and said, Father Abraham, have mercy on me, and send Lazarus, that he may dip the tip of his finger in water, and cool my tongue; for I am tormented in this flame.*—LUKE 16:22–24

Scripture plainly states that those who do not trust Christ as Saviour will spend eternity in a real lake of fire, and those who receive Christ's gift of salvation will spend eternity in Heaven.

> *And whosoever was not found written in the book of life was cast into the lake of fire.*—REVELATION 20:15

> *Blessed be the God and Father of our Lord Jesus Christ, which according to his abundant mercy hath begotten us again unto a lively hope by the resurrection of Jesus Christ from the dead, To an inheritance incorruptible, and undefiled, and that fadeth not away, reserved in heaven for you, Who are kept by the power of God through faith unto salvation ready to be revealed in the last time.*—1 PETER 1:3–5

Just as lost people tend to forget that they have an eternal soul, Christians tend to forget that every single person—family, friends, neighbors, co-workers, the grocery checkout clerk, the guy walking his dog, every person—will spend eternity in either Heaven or Hell. When we remember these eternal realities, we are much more likely to tell others the way of salvation.

JESUS IS THE ONLY WAY OF SALVATION

The Welsh poet and pastor John Dyer wrote, "A man may go to heaven without health, without riches, without honors, without learning, without friends; but he can never go there without Christ." If you are saved, there was a time in your life when you realized Christ was your only hope of salvation. You turned from your efforts to save yourself and trusted in Christ.

But we live in a pluralistic society that bristles at Christ's claim of exclusivity. "Jesus saith unto him, I am the way, the truth, and the life: no man cometh unto the Father, but by me" (John 14:6).

Most people don't mind if Christians are content to be one of many valid options in the spiritual shopping catalog. But when we stand with Peter and declare, "Neither is there salvation in any other: for there is none other name under heaven given among men, whereby we must be saved" (Acts 4:12), the world objects.

In the midst of a world that says, "All roads lead to Heaven," it's easy to want to bend our message, agreeing with people we love. But the fact is, Christ is the *only* way to Heaven, and, as we'll see in Chapter 2, you and I are responsible to share that message with others.

YOU CAN MAKE A DIFFERENCE

If we will be a consistent witness for Christ, we must allow these convictions—that every person has an eternal soul, that Heaven and Hell are real, and that Jesus is the only way to Heaven—to grip our hearts. We must believe them, remember them, and learn to see people—not as masses, not as simply personalities, but as individuals each of whom has an eternal soul that will live somewhere forever.

When we remember these truths, we'll be more likely to recognize the value of each person and to invest ourselves in making a difference by going to them with the gospel message.

CHAPTER TWO

To Seek and to Save

If you had fewer than twenty words to give a one-sentence purpose statement for your life, what would you say?

Would you list your roles? "To be the best parent, nurse, and friend I can be…"

Would you list your goals? "To find a cure for cancer by…."

Would you list the people you hope to influence?

The way you hope to be remembered?

Jesus gave His purpose statement in a succinct sixteen-word sentence: "For the Son of man is come to seek and to save that which was lost" (Luke 19:10).

This was the heartbeat of Christ. Jesus didn't come to earth to be admired or recognized, and He certainly didn't come to enjoy comfort. He had all of that in Heaven. He came for lost souls—to seek and to save the lost.

In His earthly ministry, Jesus devoted His time to those who knew they needed salvation. When the Pharisees criticized Him for spending time with those who had a sinful reputation, He replied, "They that are whole have no need of the physician, but they that are sick: I came not to call the righteous, but sinners to repentance" (Mark 2:17).

Jesus also was willing to completely rearrange His schedule to reach people with the gospel. We see Him going out of His way to talk to the woman at the well (John 4). We see Him pause what He was doing and the entire procession following Him to speak with and ultimately heal blind Bartimaeus (Mark 10:46–52). We see Him seek out people who could not come to Him, such as the crippled man by the pool of Bethesda (John 5:2–9). In short, Jesus structured His life around reaching people with the gospel.

Ultimately, Jesus came to give His life for our sins. "For even the Son of man came not to be ministered unto, but to minister, *and to give his life a ransom for many*" (Mark 10:45). Of course, Jesus did this when He shed His blood for us on the cross and then rose three days later.

But before Jesus ascended to Heaven, He left us with instructions to reach the world with the message of the gospel. We call these verses the "Great Commission."

> *And Jesus came and spake unto them, saying, All power is given unto me in heaven and in earth. Go ye therefore, and teach all nations, baptizing them in the name of the Father, and of the Son, and of the Holy Ghost: Teaching them to observe all things*

whatsoever I have commanded you: and, lo, I am
with you alway, even unto the end of the world. Amen.
—Matthew 28:18–20

These instructions have four parts:

GO

All power is given unto me in heaven and in earth. Go
ye therefore...

Notice that this command is prefaced with and based on a significant statement: "All power is given unto me in heaven and in earth."

Christ Himself tells us that He has all power. The word Jesus used for *power* is the Greek word *exousia,* and its definition refers not only to power in the sense of *might* but also power in the sense of *authority.* So before Christ gives the command to go with the gospel, He tells us, "I have all might and all authority—therefore [because of that], go!"

When we purpose to go with the gospel, we do it with the assurance that all the power of God is behind us. And when we *don't* go with the gospel, we're doing it against the authority and command of Christ.

This command involves action—you can't *go* while doing nothing. Jesus isn't just asking us to make a mental assent that people need the gospel, and He's not telling us simply to be part of a church that is reaching out with the gospel. He is calling us to personal action—to go to people who are lost and tell them how they can be saved.

If you've been saved very long, you know that, for the most part, people don't come to you and ask you how to be saved. This is why Christ instructs us to *go* to them.

WIN

...and teach all nations...

There are two times in the Great Commission where the word *teach* is used. The first time, it refers to teaching the gospel itself.

The parallel passage in Mark 16:15, uses the word *preach*: "And he said unto them, Go ye into all the world, and preach the gospel to every creature."

So not only do we go to people who are lost with the gospel, but we go with the intent to lead them to Christ. We'll look specifically at how to do that in Parts 2 and 3 of this book.

BAPTIZE

...baptizing them in the name of the Father, and of the Son, and of the Holy Ghost...

Our job doesn't end the moment someone trusts Christ as Saviour. In fact, that's when it just begins! After we have the privilege of leading someone to Christ, we need to instruct them in believers' baptism and help them take this first step of obedience in their Christian life. We'll look at what the Bible says about baptism and how to lead a new Christian in this important step in Part 4.

TEACH

...Teaching them to observe all things whatsoever I have commanded you: and, lo, I am with you alway, even unto the end of the world. Amen.

Here we come to the second time *teach* is used in the Great Commission. This time it is not about teaching the gospel itself but teaching a new believer how to live the Christian life.

When we trust Christ as our Saviour, we don't automatically know everything about Christian living or all the truths of God's Word or how to walk with the Lord or what it means to be part of a church family or...almost anything. Just like a newborn baby needs nourishing care and years of teaching to develop into a successful adult, so a new believer needs others to teach them biblical truths to develop into a mature Christian. This is so needed, in fact, that it is part of what Christ gave us in the Great Commission. We'll look at this briefly in Part 4 as well.

EMBRACING THE MISSION

Even as Jesus began the Great Commission with a statement about His power, He ends it with a promise about His presence: "Lo, I am with you alway, even unto the end of the world."

Lo is an old English interjection that means, "Look! See!" It's Christ's way of emphasizing and drawing attention to the statement He is about to make.

It's a good thing to draw our attention to Christ's promised presence. If we had to do the Great Commission alone, the task would be out of our reach. I can't convince someone of their need for salvation. I can't "save" someone, and I sure can't bring spiritual growth in another person's life. And neither can you.

But we have the promise that Christ will be with us in this endeavor.

So what would happen if you embraced this commission? If you recognized the value of a single soul and the reality of Christ's command to personally engage in going to people with the gospel? How could you make a difference through obeying the Great Commission?

In our next chapter, we'll look at what it takes to own this commission personally.

CHAPTER THREE

Owning the Mission

I heard about a deacon who had fallen into the habit of using the same phrases over and over as he led prayers in church. One day as he prayed, he said, as he did in every public prayer, "Oh Lord, touch the unsaved with Thy finger."

On this occasion, however, he suddenly stopped and fell silent. After a few seconds people began looking to see what had happened. When he continued to stand there without saying anything, someone finally went up and asked if he was not feeling well.

"No," he replied, "it's just that something seemed to say to me, 'Thou art the finger.'"

Every born again child of God wants others to be saved. Every Christian who is walking with the Lord believes in the Great Commission and wants it to be obeyed. But sometimes we forget that *we* are the ones who are supposed to obey it. This isn't a hypothetical wish that Jesus stated; it's a personal command. As Hudson Taylor, nineteenth century missionary to China, said, "The Great Commission isn't an option to be considered; it's a command to be obeyed."

In other words, "Thou art the finger."

So, if you are convinced that you personally are to engage in the Great Commission, what does it take to do it? If you were to personally own this mission, what would that look like in your life?

MAKE A COMMITMENT

The evangelist D.L. Moody used to tell the story of a lady who came to him criticizing his methods of attempting to win people to the Lord. Moody had only received a fifth-grade education, had poor English skills, and was aggressive in seeking people out and pointedly asking them if they were saved. God blessed his preaching and witnessing ministries greatly, but some people took offense at his style.

Moody's reply to this critic was gracious. "I agree with you. I don't like the way I do it either. Tell me, how do you do it?"

"I don't do it."

"Then I like my way of doing it better than your way of not doing it."

Throughout the rest of this book, we'll look at strategies and methods for how to reach people with the gospel. We'll unpack the *how* behind the four parts of the Great Commission that we saw in our last chapter.

But the *how* means little if we haven't committed to the *what*.

Remember the four words we looked at in the previous chapter—go, win, baptize, teach? These are all verbs—they require action on our part.

I'd encourage you even to pause now and make a decision that you will personally own the Great Commission. Commit to the Lord that beyond your being a part of your church or your giving to support missionaries, that you *personally* are going to share the gospel with people who are lost.

SET A PLAN

If you're like me, you have a long to-do list representing many responsibilities and commitments. And if you're like me, not all of your to-do list gets completed. We all face a constant tension between what is urgent and important, and often the most important, precious responsibilities of life get pushed to the side as we scramble to keep up with the urgent.

I've discovered, however, that what gets scheduled, gets done. For instance, my relationship with my wife, Terrie, is the dearest relationship in the world to me. I love spending time with her, and I believe having regular times together is vital to keeping our marriage strong. But if we don't specifically schedule time together, other matters of urgency keep crowding our schedules, and before long, we realize we haven't made time for just the two of us in too long.

Likewise, I believe that sharing the gospel with the lost is one of the highest priorities of the Christian life. But if I don't schedule time for it, I'll find my time filled with other pressing commitments and responsibilities. This is why for years I have had a practice of blocking off time at least once a week to go into the community and personally share the gospel.

Jesus Himself was intentional about preaching the gospel. He planned specific times and sent His disciples out with specific places in mind. You could say He had the first "organized outreach" as He sent the disciples out in groups of two with the purpose of speaking to people about their need for Christ: "After these things the Lord appointed other seventy also, and sent them two and two before his face into every city and place, whither he himself would come" (Luke 10:1).

In our church, we have multiple times each week when we provide opportunities for our church family to meet at a set location, pair up with another person from our church, receive outreach materials and a designated area or specific visits, and share the gospel. This allows people to schedule a specific time to go and even have another person to go with.

So take a moment and set a plan. What day of the week and time of day will you go out? Who will you go with? If you're new to sharing the gospel, ask someone more experienced if they would take you with them and train you. If you're experienced, look for someone who hasn't gone before, and invite them to come with you. If you aren't sure how to get involved, ask your pastor or the person in charge of outreach at your church.

SEEK GOD'S HELP

One of the jobs I worked to pay my way through Bible college was selling men's shoes at a large department store. My payment was based on commission, so I was always working to hone my techniques to make the best sales.

When it comes to sharing the gospel, it's important to be able to clearly explain salvation, and it's helpful to learn questions or statements that bring people to consider spiritual truth. But ultimately, we need the help of the Holy Spirit. Witnessing is not salesmanship; it's dependent on the power of God.

The Apostle Paul explained that he avoided "trickery" in the gospel message. He was passionate in sharing the gospel, but he didn't coerce people into professing an insincere decision:

> *For our exhortation was not of deceit, nor of uncleanness, nor in guile: But as we were allowed of God to be put in trust with the gospel, even so we speak; not as pleasing men, but God, which trieth our hearts. For neither at any time used we flattering words, as ye know, nor a cloke of covetousness; God is witness:*—1 THESSALONIANS 2:3–5

Sometimes we use the word *soulwinning* to refer to leading—or winning over—a soul to Christ. We get the word from Proverbs 11:30: "The fruit of the righteous is a tree of life; and he that winneth souls is wise."

Ultimately, however, we recognize that, while we may be "soulwinners" in a human sense, the Holy Spirit is the true Soulwinner. Only He can convince lost souls of their need for salvation, of the penalty for sin, and to put their faith in Christ (John 16:8–11). We need His power when we witness.

Paul had learned to rely on the power of the Holy Spirit: "For our gospel came not unto you in word only, but also in power, and in the Holy Ghost, and in much assurance…" (1 Thessalonians 1:5).

This point is so vital that we will revisit it throughout this book.

PREPARE A MESSAGE

One of the reasons many people hold back from sharing the gospel is that they're not quite sure what to say. If you've trusted Christ as your Saviour, you *know* the gospel—that Jesus died for your sins, rose from the dead, and gave you salvation when you called upon Him to save you (1 Corinthians 15:3–4). But describing that to someone else can feel overwhelming.

How do you begin the conversation? How do you communicate your message clearly so there is no misunderstanding? How do you know if there is misunderstanding? How do you lead someone from mere mental assent to a personal decision to receive Christ?

These are the topics we'll look at in Part 2. First, we'll define the gospel itself and then look at a sample way you can share it with a lost person, as well as how to encourage that person to make a decision for Christ.

But remember, the Great Commission begins with the command to *go*. No amount of knowledge of how to share the gospel can compensate for a lack of engagement in doing it. And, once more, before you read on, I'd like to encourage you to pause and commit to being a Christian who *goes* with the gospel.

PART TWO

Presenting the Gospel

One of the most immediate and intense desires of a new Christian is to share the incredible gift of salvation with someone else. I've seen it time and again—from my own children wanting their brothers and sisters to be saved, to newly saved adults wanting their friends and families to hear the gospel.

Anyone who has been saved can tell someone else what they experienced—even if they don't know the most polished way to present it. And almost anyone will do better than the newly-saved barber I heard about who wanted to share his faith and witness to the lost—who better than to his customers?

The next morning, his first customer came in and asked for a shave. As the barber lathered the shaving cream, he searched for the right words and tried to muster up the courage to speak. Finally, as he stood with his razor poised over the man's throat, he asked, "Are you prepared to meet God?"

You may not always find exactly the right words, but God has given you and every other Christian the task of representing Him to a lost and dying world. He tells us we are His ambassadors, responsible to take the message of salvation to others. In fact, we are standing in the stead of Christ Himself offering them salvation: "Now then we are ambassadors for Christ, as though God did beseech you by us: we pray you in Christ's stead, be ye reconciled to God" (2 Corinthians 5:20).

Thankfully, the message of the gospel is simple—Jesus died for our sins and offers us the gift of eternal life. But we must take care to present this message clearly and even convincingly, just as a government ambassador does his best to represent his country, presenting the messages with which he has been entrusted.

In this section, we'll look at the simplicity of the gospel, a skeleton outline you can use to present it, and some basic tips for witnessing.

CHAPTER FOUR

Sharing the Gospel

When I was first beginning to preach, I was out doorknocking in Coachella, California. It was over one hundred degrees that afternoon as I went house to house inviting people to our small, new church and looking for opportunities to share the gospel.

I approached a house with an open gate and knocked on the door. No one answered, but I could hear someone in the backyard, and so I decided to walk around to the other side of the house and see if I could talk to someone.

That's when I met Carl. He was standing by his garden eating, of all things, raw onions. And by *eating*, I mean he was biting off whole chunks to chew and swallow—like you might eat an apple.

I introduced myself, and Carl offered me an onion. I wasn't quite sure what to do. I had no desire to eat an onion. But on the other hand, I wanted to gain a hearing with Carl to be able to share the gospel.

I took a bite, and he offered me a seat at his picnic table.

We ate onions and chatted about gardening for a few minutes, and then I explained why I was there and invited him to our church. Soon, I was able to share the gospel with him.

Carl had a lot of questions. He had a church background that likened emotionalism to salvation, and he thought being saved was an experience that happened to a person rather than a decision they made.

But as I shared with Carl the truth from God's Word about Christ's payment for our sins on the cross and what it means to be born again, he bowed his head and trusted Christ as his Saviour right there in his backyard.

A few weeks later, I had the privilege of baptizing Carl at a special baptismal service we held at the community pool. In a short time, Carl became one of our most faithful members and soon began serving in some of the ministry opportunities of our church.

Today, Carl is in Heaven, and I'm so thankful for a hot, muggy afternoon when I got to sit at his picnic table, eat a whole raw onion, and share the gospel.

God has given us a message that is a matter of life and death to share with the world. This message is worth every effort on our part. And it is essential that we both understand it thoroughly and communicate it clearly.

In this chapter, we'll look at this message and one of the most basic presentations for sharing it with others. In our next chapter, we'll look in more depth at additional Scriptures addressing common questions people have.

UNDERSTANDING THE GOSPEL

Before you can clearly share the gospel with someone else, you need to be clear on what the gospel is—and isn't.

Sometimes people see church outreach merely as an opportunity to show kindness to others, such as by doing projects to serve the community. Or they think of it as a way to sway people's political views or change their perceptions of God and the church. Our purpose, however, is to share a singularly focused message—the gospel. Creating opportunities to communicate that message may include showing kindness or serving others. But sharing the gospel itself is sharing the death, burial, and resurrection of Christ.

We see this in 1 Corinthians 15, where Paul clearly defines the gospel:

> *Moreover, brethren, I declare unto you the gospel which I preached unto you…For I delivered unto you first of all that which I also received, how that Christ died for our sins according to the scriptures; And that he was buried, and that he rose again the third day according to the scriptures:*—1 CORINTHIANS 15:1, 3–4

That's it! That is the gospel. It is the death, burial, and resurrection of Christ for our sins.

The word *gospel* literally means "good news." Indeed, Christ's death in our stead, His burial, and His triumphant victory over the grave *is* good news! By placing our trust in Him and in the payment He already paid for our sins, we are reconciled to God and given a home in Heaven.

This is the message we have been commissioned to share with others. It is our job to make our message crystal clear so that there will be no misunderstanding.

How do we do that?

Avoid the Extremes

Some people complicate the gospel. They so front-load it with elaborate terminology and extra-biblical requirements that it becomes more of a discussion point among mature Christians than a gospel invitation to the lost. It seems some Christians expect an above-average emotional display combined with deep theological knowledge on the part of the lost man in order to be convinced he is truly converted. In truth, volumes could be written on the doctrine of salvation. But those of us who have shared the gospel with lost people and have seen many come to Christ know that no one understands all the theology behind salvation the day they are saved, nor do they need to. They simply need to understand that Jesus died and rose for their sins and turn in faith to Christ.

While some soulwinners complicate the message, others make it shallow. They are repetitive and trite in their presentation, making it more of a sales pitch to "pray a prayer" than a call to turn to and believe solely in Christ for salvation.

Before a person can be saved, they must fully understand that they are a sinner in need of a Saviour and turn repentantly to Christ in faith. Acts 20:21 gives us an understanding of how repentance relates to salvation: "Testifying both to the Jews, and also to the Greeks, **repentance** toward God, and **faith** toward our Lord Jesus Christ."

Repentance and faith are two sides of the same coin. *Repentance* means to turn around and go in the opposite direction. A person repents when they realize they are a sinner deserving God's righteous judgment and that their own works can't save them. This change of mind about their hope of salvation leads them to faith in Christ. *Faith* is believing that Jesus Christ is the only means by which to be forgiven and to receive eternal life. This brings us again to a summary of the gospel—Jesus died for our sins and offers us salvation.

I don't usually use the word *repentance* when I'm witnessing to someone, because most unsaved people don't know what it means. I do, however, make sure I thoroughly explain the truth of turning from self effort and turning to Christ alone for salvation.

Both extremes—the complicated, front-loaded requirements and the shallow, trite presentations—garble the message with which we have been entrusted. We must learn to share the gospel in its pure simplicity while relying on the Holy Spirit to convict hearts and to be a true soulwinner.

Have a Plan

That said, there is a core set of verses that clearly give the main truths of the gospel—that we are sinners condemned by God, that Christ died for our sins, and that He offers us the gift of salvation.

My advice to new soulwinners is to learn and memorize these verses and to be prepared to share them with a lost person in any setting—out doorknocking, with a friend over a cup of coffee, etc. My advice to all soulwinners, however, is to let the Holy Spirit lead you in which Scriptures to use as you share the gospel. While having a starting place is important, and the Scriptures I'll give here are a clear way to share the gospel, realize that the Holy Spirit will sometimes lead you to use other Scriptures. In Chapter 5, we'll look at additional verses related to salvation as well as common questions and biblical answers. But, for a basic framework, the five main truths and the verses in this section provide a good start for sharing the gospel with someone who is lost.

GIVING A CLEAR PRESENTATION

So, how do you present it? In our next chapter, we'll look at sample scenarios and suggested ways to lead into a gospel conversation. But assuming you're at the point where you are ready to present the gospel, what would that look like?

What follows is more or less my basic gospel presentation. You don't need to memorize or use my exact words; I'm simply providing them as a sample of how you can share the gospel, explaining each verse and moving from one Scripture to the next.

I will often ask the person to whom I'm speaking a question to move from small talk to spiritual dialog. Depending on the context of the situation, I may ask, "Has anyone shown you from the Bible how you can know without a doubt you are on your way to Heaven?" or "If you were to die today, do you know if you would go to Heaven or Hell, or do you know?" If they are not sure, I ask if they will allow me a few moments to share what the Bible says. Along the way, I try to remain sensitive to whether or not they are responding to each truth I'm sharing and to allow the Holy Spirit to direct me to other passages or even to continue the conversation at another time.

From here, I'll add comments to you in parentheses, but the rest of the text is how I would explain the basic truths of salvation to whom I'm witnessing.

Understand that God loves you.

The first thing that you need to understand is that God loves you. He loves you so much that He gave Himself for you.

> *For God so loved the world, that he gave his only begotten Son, that whosoever believeth in him should not perish, but have everlasting life.*—JOHN 3:16

But that's not all. God not only loves you; He wants you to know that you can have a home in Heaven with Him. Some people think we can only *hope* we will be in Heaven. But God wants us to *know*.

> *These things have I written unto you that believe on the name of the Son of God; that ye may **know** that ye have eternal life, and that ye may believe on the name of the Son of God.*—1 JOHN 5:13

(If I'm talking to someone who is of a background, especially Catholic, where they seem hesitant that someone could really know they are going to Heaven, I'll often pause as I come to the word *know* in 1 John 5:13 and ask them to read it, to emphasize its significance to them.)

So, if God loves us and wants us to know we have eternal life, why doesn't everyone automatically go to Heaven? That's what we have to understand next.

Realize your condition.

The Bible tells us that we are all lost in sin. Sin is any act contrary to God's laws and commandments, and all of us sin.

Romans 5:12 teaches us that since Adam and Eve, the first man and woman on earth, a sin nature has been present in all people: "Wherefore, as by one man sin entered into the world, and death by sin; and so death passed upon all men, for that all have sinned." No one had to teach us how to sin; sinning comes naturally to us.

But the Bible teaches that our sin separates us from God. *As it is written, There is none righteous, no, not one:* —ROMANS 3:10

For all have sinned, and come short of the glory of God;—ROMANS 3:23

Notice God's price for sin.

For the wages of sin is death; but the gift of God is eternal life through Jesus Christ our Lord. —ROMANS 6:23

A wage is what you earn for what you do. For instance, a man earns a paycheck for the work he has done. Even so, we deserve eternal death in Hell for the sins we have committed.

Some people believe they can pay the price for sin by doing good works or being involved in religion. This may seem logical, but it's not what the Bible says. In fact, the Bible specifically tells us that we *can't* earn our way to Heaven through good works.

For by grace are ye saved through faith; and that not of yourselves: it is the gift of God: not of works, lest any man should boast.—EPHESIANS 2:8–9

Believe Christ died for you.

Though we deserve eternal death for our sin, Jesus paid our payment when He died for us. We were lost and separated from God, but He loved us. Because He is love, He sent His own Son—Jesus Christ—to die on the cross for our sin. After His death, He rose from the dead three days later.

John 3:16 explains, "For God so loved the world, that he gave his only begotten Son, that whosoever believeth in him should not perish, but have everlasting life."

As Romans 6:23 tells us, Christ now offers us the gift of eternal life: "…the gift of God is eternal life through Jesus Christ our Lord." This is a gift Christ paid for when He died for our sins. Through His death and resurrection, Jesus became the payment for our sin. Now we do not have to pay for our sin ourselves. By His grace, salvation is provided.

> *But God commendeth [showed] his love toward us, in that, while we were yet sinners, Christ died for us.*
> —ROMANS 5:8

Confess your faith in Christ.

To have a relationship with God and an eternal home in Heaven, we must stop trusting ourselves, our works, or our religion and place our full trust in the Lord Jesus Christ alone for forgiveness of our sin and for eternal life.

> *That if thou shalt confess with thy mouth the Lord Jesus, and shalt believe in thine heart that God hath raised him from the dead, thou shalt be saved. For with the heart man believeth unto righteousness; and with the mouth confession is made unto salvation. For the scripture saith, Whosoever believeth on him shall not be ashamed.*—ROMANS 10:9–11

To "be saved" speaks of being saved from the penalty of our sins—eternal separation from God in Hell. Although we are sinners separated from God, Jesus Christ—the perfect, sinless, Son of God—provided the way of salvation.

Another way God helps us understand this is in John 3:7, where Jesus said, "Ye must be born again." To be "born again" is to be born into God's family—to have a spiritual birth date when we turn from trusting in ourselves or our religion and place our trust in Jesus and His sacrifice for our sins. It is when we in faith call on the Lord to save us.

God Himself promises that if you realize your sinful condition and confess Christ as your Saviour, trusting the payment He made for your sin and turning to Him alone to be your Saviour, He will save you.

> *For whosoever shall call upon the name of the Lord shall be saved.*—ROMANS 10:13

LEADING TO A DECISION

I don't just want to "share" the gospel—as in, get the word out. I want to see the person to whom I am speaking trust Christ as Saviour. So how do I lead this person to a decision?

At this point in our conversation, I am very sensitive to how the person is responding. If he has been attentive and it seems the Holy Spirit is working conviction in his heart, I'll continue our conversation by inviting him to call on the Lord Jesus by faith for salvation. But if he's distracted and only giving cursory mental assent to these truths, I'll likely pull back and give the Holy Spirit time to work in his heart. I'll still try to keep in contact with him, and I'll look for another opportunity to witness to him.

If I continue, I'll likely ask a few summary questions, something like the following:

- Do you believe that you are a sinner, separated from God, and without the ability to save yourself?

- Do you believe that Jesus, God's Son, shed His blood to pay for your sin?

- Would there be anything that would keep you from turning to and trusting in Jesus Christ as your Saviour today?

- As we saw a moment ago, God promises, "That if thou shalt confess with thy mouth the Lord Jesus, and shalt believe in thine heart that God hath raised him from the dead, thou shalt be saved. For with the heart man believeth unto righteousness; and with the mouth confession is made unto salvation. For whosoever shall call upon the name of the Lord shall be saved" (Romans 10:9–10, 13).

- Even as you "confess with your mouth" that you are putting your trust in Christ, it is important that you also "believe in your heart." It is the faith of your heart that saves you.

Once again, I'm careful to observe how the person is responding and to ask the Holy Spirit to help me discern if He is working in his heart. Typically, I ask, "Would you like to turn to Christ in faith and call on the Lord for salvation now?"

If the person responds with hesitation, I ask what would keep them from turning to Christ. I'm always so aware at this point of my dependence on the Holy Spirit. If they have sincere questions, I want to respond with wisdom. (We'll look at some of the common questions in Chapter 6.) But if they need to be urged to trust Christ—like someone who is fearful would be urged to jump from a burning building into a rescue net—I want to urge them to not delay a decision.

Often, however, if I've gotten to this point in a conversation with someone showing genuine interest and I ask them if they'd like to turn to Christ for salvation now, they often respond with a "yes." Usually, I will review the gospel presentation in the form of a sample prayer. I might say something like, "That's wonderful, Joe. Why don't you call out to Christ right now to save you? Simply confess to Him that you are a sinner and ask Him, as the Son of God, to cleanse you and be your Saviour. Remember, you're talking to God, not to me. I'll pray after you."

Occasionally, if the person seems hesitant to pray because they don't feel like they know how to pray or what they would say, I lead them in a prayer, allowing them to repeat after me. I always stress that they are praying to God, not to me, and that they need to mean it from their heart. If I lead them in a prayer, I suggest using something like this:

Dear Lord, I know that I am separated from you because of sin. I confess that in my sin I cannot save myself. Right now, I turn to you alone to be my Saviour. I ask you to save me from the penalty of my sin, and I trust you to provide eternal life to me. Amen.

PREPARING TO SHARE THE GOSPEL

So there it is in a nutshell—a basic gospel presentation. If you have never led someone to Christ, I would encourage you to do three things.

1. Reread this chapter a few times. Don't memorize the exact words, but get a sense of how you can present the main Scriptures clearly and how you can transition from one to the next.

2. Practice presenting the gospel. With just the main points and the verses (as below) pretend *you* are presenting the gospel to someone else. Practice talking through it aloud several times. You'll be surprised at how that will help prepare you for an opportunity when you can share your faith.

- **Understand that God loves you.**
  For God so loved the world, that he gave his only begotten Son, that whosoever believeth in him should not perish, but have everlasting life.—JOHN 3:16

- **Realize your condition.**
  As it is written, There is none righteous, no, not one:—ROMANS 3:10

For all have sinned, and come short of the glory of God;—ROMANS 3:23

- **Notice God's price for sin.**
  For the wages of sin is death; but the gift of God is eternal life through Jesus Christ our Lord.—ROMANS 6:23

  For by grace are ye saved through faith; and that not of yourselves: it is the gift of God: not of works, lest any man should boast.—EPHESIANS 2:8–9

- **Believe Christ died for you.**
  But God commendeth [showed] his love toward us, in that, while we were yet sinners, Christ died for us.—ROMANS 5:8

- **Confess your faith in Christ.**
  That if thou shalt confess with thy mouth the Lord Jesus, and shalt believe in thine heart that God hath raised him from the dead, thou shalt be saved. For with the heart man believeth unto righteousness; and with the mouth confession is made unto salvation. For the scripture saith, Whosoever believeth on him shall not be ashamed.—ROMANS 10:9–11

  For whosoever shall call upon the name of the Lord shall be saved.—ROMANS 10:13

3. Be prepared to share the gospel with others. Practice looking up these verses in your New Testament or even mark them so they are easy to find. It's helpful when you are sharing the gospel with someone if you *show* them the verses in the

Bible, rather than simply quoting them. This allows the person to see that what you are telling them really does come from God's Word.

Sometimes you may find that sharing your own testimony helps as you share the gospel with someone else.

Of course, people aren't saved simply because you and I *know* the gospel. They are saved when we *go* to them with the gospel. In speaking of the necessity of bringing the good news of salvation to the lost, Romans 10:17 says, "So then faith cometh by hearing, and hearing by the word of God." In our next chapter, let's look at some sample conversations for leading into a gospel presentation.

CHAPTER FIVE

Dealing with Common Questions

I t's probably every new soulwinner's greatest fear—what if someone asks me a question to which I don't know the answer?

Let me put your fear to rest—it will happen. *And it's okay.* If you wait to witness until you know the Bible answer to every conceivable question, you'll never share the gospel until you get to Heaven. (And the people there already know it.)

It is good, however, to be familiar with answers to some of the most common questions people ask. In this chapter, we'll look at some of these, including a significant look at how we know Jesus is God in the flesh.

If you are a brand new soulwinner, don't feel like you need to memorize all of these verses. Simply read them so you are familiar with them, and as you gain experience, you'll have opportunities to refer back to them.

COMMON OBJECTIONS

Below are some commonly asked questions or statements people may ask to someone sharing the gospel with them, as well as some verses that address those areas.

"I have always been a Christian."

No one is born a Christian. Even if a person is born into a home with Christian parents or is baptized into a church as a baby, he or she must make a personal choice to trust Christ to be saved.

> Behold, I was shapen in iniquity; and in sin did my mother conceive me.—PSALM 51:5

> But as many as received him, to them gave he power to become the sons of God, even to them that believe on his name:—JOHN 1:12

> Jesus answered and said unto him, Verily, verily, I say unto thee, Except a man be born again, he cannot see the kingdom of God.—JOHN 3:3

"I've asked God to forgive me many times."

Another variant of this is, "I pray every day." The soulwinner should explain that praying to receive Christ as Saviour is different than just repeated prayer. It is a prayer of faith, believing in Christ's ability and willingness to save, and is a one-time decision.

> *But as many as received him, to them gave he power to become the sons of God, even to them that believe on his name:*—JOHN 1:12

> *For whosoever shall call upon the name of the Lord shall be saved.*—ROMANS 10:13

> *Behold, I stand at the door, and knock: if any man hear my voice, and open the door, I will come in to him, and will sup with him, and he with me.* —REVELATION 3:20

"This is too simple. I need to do something to earn it."

If we could earn salvation, it wouldn't be a gift. If it could be partly our effort and partly God's grace, it wouldn't be grace at all.

> *For the wages of sin is death; but the gift of God is eternal life through Jesus Christ our Lord.* —ROMANS 6:23

> *For by grace are ye saved through faith; and that not of yourselves: it is the gift of God: Not of works, lest any man should boast.*—EPHESIANS 2:8–9

> *Not by works of righteousness which we have done, but according to his mercy he saved us, by the washing*

of regeneration, and renewing of the Holy Ghost;
—TITUS 3:5

"I'm good enough. I'm not a very bad sinner."

We might look good compared to another person, but compared to God, we are in desperate need of salvation.

> *All we like sheep have gone astray; we have turned every one to his own way; and the LORD hath laid on him the iniquity of us all.*—ISAIAH 53:6

> *But we are all as an unclean thing, and all our righteousnesses are as filthy rags; and we all do fade as a leaf; and our iniquities, like the wind, have taken us away.*—ISAIAH 64:6

> *They are all gone out of the way, they are together become unprofitable; there is none that doeth good, no, not one.*—ROMANS 3:12

"Doesn't death end everything? How do we know there is a real Heaven and Hell?"

Some people believe that death ends everything, but the Bible plainly speaks of our eternal soul and of a real Heaven and Hell.

> *And as it is appointed unto men once to die, but after this the judgment:*—HEBREWS 9:27

> *After this manner therefore pray ye: Our Father which art in heaven, Hallowed be thy name.*—MATTHEW 6:9

And it came to pass, that the beggar died, and was carried by the angels into Abraham's bosom: the rich man also died, and was buried; And in hell he lift up his eyes, being in torments, and seeth Abraham afar off, and Lazarus in his bosom. And he cried and said, Father Abraham, have mercy on me, and send Lazarus, that he may dip the tip of his finger in water, and cool my tongue; for I am tormented in this flame.—LUKE 16:22–24

"I don't want to give up my lifestyle or my friends."

There is nothing more valuable than your eternal soul. When you trust Christ as your Saviour, He will give you the grace to desire a new life and be able to live a new life.

For what shall it profit a man, if he shall gain the whole world, and lose his own soul? Or what shall a man give in exchange for his soul?—MARK 8:36–37

Greater love hath no man than this, that a man lay down his life for his friends.—JOHN 15:13

For it is God which worketh in you both to will and to do of his good pleasure.—PHILIPPIANS 2:13

"I think as long as I'm sincere in what I believe, that's all that matters."

There is a way which seemeth right unto a man, but the end thereof are the ways of death.—PROVERBS 14:12

He that believeth on the Son hath everlasting life: and he that believeth not the Son shall not see life; but the wrath of God abideth on him.—John 3:36

Jesus saith unto him, I am the way, the truth, and the life: no man cometh unto the Father, but by me. —John 14:6

Neither is there salvation in any other: for there is none other name under heaven given among men, whereby we must be saved.—Acts 4:12

He that hath the Son hath life; and he that hath not the Son of God hath not life.—1 John 5:12

THE DEITY OF CHRIST

One of the most important truths for a soulwinner—for every Christian—is to have a firm grasp on the deity of Christ. False teachers and cults all attack the truth that Jesus is, in fact, God.

Why is this so important? Because if Jesus is not God, that would mean He did not live a sinless life, and He could not pay for our sins. Also, if Jesus is not God, His sacrifice could not cover the sins of the entire world. But Scripture specifically states both are true.

And ye know that he was manifested to take away our sins; and in him is no sin.—1 John 3:5

And he is the propitiation for our sins: and not for ours only, but also for the sins of the whole world. —1 John 2:2

The Bible also tells us that those who teach that Jesus is not God are false teachers.

> *And every spirit that confesseth not that Jesus Christ is come in the flesh is not of God: and this is that spirit of antichrist, whereof ye have heard that it should come; and even now already is it in the world.*—1 JOHN 4:3

> *And without controversy great is the mystery of godliness: God was manifest in the flesh, justified in the Spirit, seen of angels, preached unto the Gentiles, believed on in the world, received up into glory.* —1 TIMOTHY 3:16

So, we know it is important that Jesus is God. But how do we know it is true?

His deity is shown through His names.

Throughout the Bible Jesus is called "God."[1]

> *For unto us a child is born, unto us a son is given: and the government shall be upon his shoulder: and his name shall be called Wonderful, Counsellor, The mighty God, The everlasting Father, The Prince of Peace.*—ISAIAH 9:6

> *And Thomas answered and said unto him, My Lord and my God.*—JOHN 20:28

---

1.   Additional references include Hebrews 1:8; 1 Timothy 3:16; Titus 2:13; Romans 9:3–5; 1 John 3:16, 5:20; Revelation 1:8, 21:6–7; Colossians 2:9.

His deity is shown through His works.

Jesus performed works that only God can do.

- He created the world.

  All things were made by him; and without him was not any thing made that was made.—JOHN 1:3

- He upholds the world.

  Who being the brightness of his glory, and the express image of his person, and upholding all things by the word of his power, when he had by himself purged our sins, sat down on the right hand of the Majesty on high;—HEBREWS 1:3

- He forgives sin.

  Why doth this man thus speak blasphemies? who can forgive sins but God only? And immediately when Jesus perceived in his spirit that they so reasoned within themselves, he said unto them, Why reason ye these things in your hearts? Whether is it easier to say to the sick of the palsy, Thy sins be forgiven thee; or to say, Arise, and take up thy bed, and walk? But that ye may know that the Son of man hath power on earth to forgive sins, (he saith to the sick of the palsy,) I say unto thee, Arise, and take up thy bed, and go thy way into thine house.—MARK 2:7–11

- He gives eternal life.

  As thou hast given him power over all flesh, that he should give eternal life to as many as thou hast given him.—JOHN 17:2

His deity is shown through worship.

The Bible tells us plainly that we are to worship God only (Luke 4:8), yet, throughout the Gospels, we see many people worship Jesus. He never stopped a single one of them.

> *Saying, Where is he that is born King of the Jews? for we have seen his star in the east, and are come to worship him.*—MATTHEW 2:2

> *Then they that were in the ship came and worshipped him, saying, Of a truth thou art the Son of God.* —MATTHEW 14:33

> *And he said, Lord, I believe. And he worshipped him.*—JOHN 9:38

We even see that God the Father commands the angels to worship Him.

> *And again, when he bringeth in the firstbegotten into the world, he saith, And let all the angels of God worship him.*—HEBREWS 1:6

His deity is shown through His attributes.

Jesus exhibits characteristics that belong to God alone. Notice just a few of these qualities:

- Omnipotence
  And Jesus came and spake unto them, saying, All power is given unto me in heaven and in earth. —MATTHEW 28:18

- Omniscience

  Now are we sure that thou knowest all things, and needest not that any man should ask thee: by this we believe that thou camest forth from God.—JOHN 16:30

  From that time forth began Jesus to shew unto his disciples, how that he must go unto Jerusalem, and suffer many things of the elders and chief priests and scribes, and be killed, and be raised again the third day.—MATTHEW 16:21

- Omnipresence

  …and, lo, I am with you alway, even unto the end of the world. Amen.—MATTHEW 28:20

- Eternality

  In the beginning was the Word, and the Word was with God, and the Word was God.—JOHN 1:1

- Immutability

  Jesus Christ the same yesterday, and to day, and for ever.—HEBREWS 13:8

His deity is shown through His resurrection.

The most spectacular evidence of Jesus' deity was His bodily resurrection from the dead. Indeed, the resurrection of Jesus Christ is, as one man put it, "the crowning proof of Christianity."[2]

---

2. Henry M. Morris, *Many Infallible Proofs: Evidences for the Christian Faith* (New Leaf Publishing Group, 1974), 97.

*Now upon the first day of the week, very early in the morning, they came unto the sepulchre, bringing the spices which they had prepared, and certain others with them. And they found the stone rolled away from the sepulchre. And they entered in, and found not the body of the Lord Jesus. And it came to pass, as they were much perplexed thereabout, behold, two men stood by them in shining garments: And as they were afraid, and bowed down their faces to the earth, they said unto them, Why seek ye the living among the dead? He is not here, but is risen: remember how he spake unto you when he was yet in Galilee, Saying, The Son of man must be delivered into the hands of sinful men, and be crucified, and the third day rise again.—*LUKE 24:1–7

Jesus didn't rise from the dead secretly. Scripture records over ten different recorded appearances of Jesus after His resurrection.[3]

Only God could raise Himself from the dead. Yes, we can be sure that Jesus is God, that His offer of salvation is good, and that He will save all who put their trust in Him.

COMMON QUESTIONS, REAL ANSWERS

In these past chapters, I've mentioned a few times that what I've given you is a basic gospel presentation and answers to common questions. I'd like to encourage you to not stop here

---

3. See John 20:11–18; Matthew 28:1–10; 1 Corinthians 15:5; Luke 24:13–35; John 20:19–24, 26–28, 21:1–23; 1 Corinthians 15:6–6; Acts 1:3–10, 9:3–9.

but to keep growing as a soulwinner and in your personal Bible knowledge. You may not always have the answer to someone's question, and it's fine to say, "That's a great question; let's talk again when I can give you an answer from the Bible"—and then get help from someone more experienced.

So use these chapters as your starting place, and continue growing and learning. In fact, one of the best ways to grow in your ability to clearly communicate the gospel is to keep sharing it. Make it your goal that you will share the gospel so often that your ability to share it clearly will develop as you rely on the Holy Spirit for guidance.

CHAPTER SIX

Making a
Soulwinning Visit

If you read through the New Testament specifically looking for each time the gospel is presented to a lost person, one of the things you'll notice is that no two presentations are exactly the same. When Peter preached at Pentecost in Acts 2, he used a different approach than Philip did when he talked to the Ethiopian man traveling through the desert in Acts 8. When Jesus talked to Nicodemus in John 3, He used a different approach than when He talked with the woman at the well in John 4.

There are times when someone will approach you and ask you questions about your faith and how they can be saved. Sometimes, as Nicodemus did with Jesus, someone will initiate a conversation with you in which you may be able to share the gospel. Praise God for these moments, and be ready to share your faith when they come.

But many times, we must be the ones to confront or initiate a conversation—such as Jesus did with the woman at the well. If Jesus had never brought up "living water" in this conversation, she would have gone to the well, given him a drink, and they both would have gone on their way. But because Jesus cared for her eternal destiny, He broke some cultural norms (a Jewish man talking to a Samaritan woman) and gently, but persistently, engaged her in gospel conversation.

Take a few moments to read through this passage, noting how Jesus engaged this woman in gospel conversation—first with "small talk," then piquing her curiosity, then giving eternal truth…all the while repeatedly bringing the conversation back on topic when she would diverge.

> *There cometh a woman of Samaria to draw water: Jesus saith unto her, Give me to drink. (For his disciples were gone away unto the city to buy meat.) Then saith the woman of Samaria unto him, How is it that thou, being a Jew, askest drink of me, which am a woman of Samaria? for the Jews have no dealings with the Samaritans. Jesus answered and said unto her, If thou knewest the gift of God, and who it is that saith to thee, Give me to drink; thou wouldest have asked of him, and he would have given thee living water.*
> —John 4:7–10

In a future chapter, we'll look specifically at witnessing to people with whom you have a pre-existing relationship—

family, friends, business acquaintances, etc. But in this chapter, we'll look at making a visit through your local church ministry, specifically for the purpose of evangelism. At the end of the chapter, we'll also touch on some basic, practical tips for these types of visits.

Once again, I'd like to reiterate that God has given us a message, not a script. In other words, our job is to effectively communicate the gospel, not to repeat specific words. And, even though in this chapter I am suggesting specific words for making soulwinning visits, I am just intending to help you get started and to provide ideas. The more regular you are in soulwinning, the easier it will be for you to adapt your approach based on the person to whom you are talking.

EXAMPLE CONVERSATIONS

Generally speaking, there are two types of visits you'll make in soulwinning that is organized through your church.

The first would be when you are knocking on all the doors in a particular area or talking to everyone who is out at a park or community event. I believe this kind of purposed outreach is needful. Acts 8:4 speaks of the early Christians who "went every where preaching the word." And in Acts 20:20, Paul said, "And how I…have shewed you, and have taught you publickly, and from house to house."

The second kind of visit would be when you're following up on a guest who attended services on Sunday or visiting the parent of a child reached through your church's outreach.

The first type of visit is more random, and the second is one in which you're going to a particular address or meeting place to talk to a specific person. This second visit may even be scheduled with a call in advance. The approaches for both are similar but a little different.

For a doorknocking or canvassing visit

I have the privilege almost every week (when I have no follow up appointments) to take a street or several streets in our community and go to each home to invite people to church and, most importantly, to look for an opportunity to share the gospel. Periodically, I will be privileged to lead someone to Christ with this approach, but nearly always, I meet someone who becomes a specific follow up visit in the future.

We often call this door-to-door soulwinning or doorknocking. How do you approach a visit like this?

Introduce yourself. State your name and if you have someone with you, their name as well. *Hi, I'm Paul, and this is my wife Terrie.* (If the person you're meeting mentions their name, do your best to remember it. If you're able to use their name throughout the rest of your conversation, it shows that you are listening and that you care.)

Clearly give the name of your church. This helps alleviate fear in my listener that I'm a Jehovah's Witness, from another cult, representing a political candidate, or am a salesman. *We're from Lancaster Baptist Church.*

Explain the purpose for your visit. Invite the person to attend services at your church and offer them a tract, outreach card, or flyer. *We're here in your neighborhood today to invite you to visit our church.*

Invite them to your church. This is a good time to ask them specifically, *Would you be my guest at church this Sunday?* If they say they have another church, don't criticize that church or ask them again to come to yours on a Sunday morning. There is something more important that you want to share with them—the gospel—so this is no place for a "church argument."

Determine if this is the right time to continue the visit. If you caught the person at an inconvenient time, it's probably best to not make it a long conversation. If you do, you'll leave them feeling frustrated with you and your church. Also, if they are obviously uninterested, as in they never opened the screen door or they are shutting the door as you talk, it's also best to leave them with a simple invitation to your church.

If you end the conversation here, simply thank them for their time and reiterate that you would love to have them visit. Make it your goal that even on a short visit, you'll accomplish the following objectives:

- Leave a tract or gospel invitation.

- Give a personal invitation for the person to visit your church.

- Create a sense in their heart that the church cares about them and can help meet their spiritual needs.

- Leave before you wear out your welcome, so that you keep the door open for a future visit.

On the other hand, if they are willing to continue talking, this is the time to turn the conversation to spiritual things.

Look for an opportunity to turn the conversation. You may need a moment of small talk first. Usually, as I'm walking up to a house, I look for something I can compliment or comment on (a manicured yard, support for a sports team, etc.) if the opportunity presents itself.

Ultimately, however, I'm looking for an opportunity to say something to turn the conversation so I can share the gospel. Depending on what they have already said to me, I may say something like this: "Joe, going to church is so important, and I'm glad you do. Ultimately, though, the most important matter for all of us is where we will spend eternity. Could I ask you, do you know for sure that you will be in Heaven?"

Often, the person will say that they don't know for sure, but they hope they will go to Heaven. That gives me the opportunity to respond, *Would you like to know?*

If they say, "Yeah, but I'm busy right now," I don't force the conversation. I usually will ask for a time when I can come back, and hopefully, I'll leave with an appointment to return. If they hesitate, I bring the conversation back to inviting them to church. This still leaves the door open for me to return and invite them again in the future. I may also ask for their phone number or email.

In the cases where they will say they would like to know how they can go to Heaven, I would present the gospel as outlined in the previous chapter.

Exchange contact information. If a conversation has gone this far—whether or not you share the gospel—this is probably someone you want to ask to take down their contact information to be able to visit again. You may offer your cell number as a sign of good faith as well.

- **If I have not shared the gospel:** *Joe, thanks for your time today. I really would love for you to visit Lancaster Baptist sometime soon. Let me give you my phone number so you can let me know which Sunday you come or if you have any questions in the meantime.* I usually write my number on the tract I gave them. As I finish writing it, I'll say, *Do you mind giving me your number as well?* As I write their number, *Do you mind if I check in with you again?* I'll either ask them for their address, or I'll just look at their house and write it down as I leave.

- **If I have shared the gospel:** *Joe, thank you again for your time today. I want to give you my phone number so you can call me with any questions.* From there, getting their number would be similar as above. If they have been saved, I'll also share assurance verses with them, which we'll look at in Chapter 11. If I've shared the gospel but they have not yet received Christ as their Saviour, I encourage them to call or text with any questions they may have, and I go back to their home later to talk with them again. On a repeat visit, I try to bring something with me—such as a little book on salvation, *Paid in Full* (available through Striving Together Publications)—to help give me a "reason" for coming and reopening the conversation.

I add the contact information that I leave with from these visits to a list that I call my prospect list. We'll come back to this list in Chapter 8.

For a specific visit

When you are making a specifically assigned visit, such as following up on a guest who visited church last Sunday or the parents of a child reached through your church's ministry, Sometimes we call ahead to set up an appointment but not always. Otherwise, much of the above notes are similar.

You introduce yourself, quickly give the name of your church, and early on explain the purpose for your visit. One difference, however, is that in this type of visit, you usually have more opportunity for casual conversation. This is helpful, because the more someone feels that you are their friend, the more likely they are to open up to you in spiritual conversation. Casual conversation helps to establish something of a friendship before you lead into sharing the gospel.

Somewhere I saw the following acrostic for HELP in getting a conversation started. This isn't a list you talk through, but simply an easy-to-remember way to think of something to compliment someone on or ask them about.

- **House**—Did you notice flowers in the yard, or is there something in the interior you can comment on? *We have the same painting in our living room.*

- **Employment**—Where do they work? What is their job like?

- **Loved ones**—How many children do they have? If you already know a family member who attends your church, you can comment on why you appreciate that person.

- **Possessions**—Do they have pets? Do you have the same car?

People like to talk about subjects that are familiar to them. Thus, taking a few minutes for small talk is helpful when you have the opportunity.

Remember, though, that if you don't have a genuine interest in people, they will know it. Beyond making small talk, ask the Lord to help you develop a real love and concern for people. Before making a specific visit, pray specifically for the people you are about to see by name.

Once again, remember that the chief goal in your visit is to present the gospel. You may be at the home to ask permission for a child to be baptized or to invite someone who attended services on Sunday to come to an adult Bible class. But you are also looking for an opportunity to turn the conversation to salvation, in a similar way as mentioned above.

It was on a specific follow-up visit that I first got to share the gospel with Steve and Pam Keller, who have been dear members of our church for over twenty-five years now. The Kellers had visited Lancaster Baptist one Sunday and then left for vacation the day after. Not knowing they were out of town, I tried visiting a few times over the next several days.

With no one home each time, I eventually decided to call ahead for an appointment. As the Lord allowed it, the day I called was the day after they returned from vacation. We set a time for me and another man from our church, Dan Migliore, to stop by and talk to Steve and Pam.

I didn't know it, but Steve had attended Baptist churches in the past but had never been personally questioned regarding his salvation testimony or had someone personally share the gospel with him. He had even been baptized without someone making sure he understood the gospel. In fact, by this time, Steve thought baptism was the link to having a relationship with God and being part of a church.

The other thing I didn't know was that before Dan and I arrived, Pam, who had been saved before she married Steve, tried to prepare Steve for our visit. "You know, they're going to ask you if you've been saved."

"Saved? They're going to ask me if I want to be baptized."

"No, they're going to ask you about being saved."

"No, this is a Baptist church. They're going to talk about being baptized."

By the time I rang the doorbell, Steve and Pam were in the thick of their discussion about what Dan and I had come to talk about.

We chatted for a few minutes about Steve's job in the Air Force, the different places they had lived around the country, and their move to our area. All the while, Steve and Pam were waiting to see what I would ask when the conversation turned to church—would it be about salvation or baptism?

After we had gotten acquainted and the conversation turned to the churches they had attended in the past, I saw my opportunity to open a gospel conversation. Because of his familiarity with churches, I phrased my question a little differently than I normally would. "Steve, you've mentioned churches you've attended. Can you tell me about when you were saved?"

Before he even answered me, he looked at Pam and said, "You were right!"

As it turned out, that evening was the first time someone had ever opened the Bible and shared with Steve how he could know Christ as his personal Saviour. As we talked through various Scriptures that evening, it was like a light bulb came on in his mind as the pieces of Bible truth he had previously heard came together into a clear picture of the gospel. He bowed his head and trusted Christ that evening in his living room.

Today, Steve and Pam are faithful members of Lancaster Baptist Church who regularly share the gospel with others. Steve even serves as a deacon, and together they teach in our children's ministry.

But think back to that visit for a moment. If I had left the Kellers' home, assuming Steve must be saved and had never asked him about his salvation, he would not have been saved that evening…and perhaps ever.

When you make a follow-up visit, remember that your main purpose is to find out if the person is saved and to be prepared to share the message of the gospel.

PRACTICAL TIPS

As we close this chapter, I'd like to note several practical tips for going out with the gospel throughout your community:

1. *Carry a New Testament with you.* A New Testament has all of the verses generally used in presenting the gospel and is not as intimidating to someone as a large Bible. Many soulwinners mark the basic Scriptures they regularly use to share the gospel in their New Testament. This makes it easy to point out specific verses to the person to whom they are witnessing. Additionally, a New Testament is easy to keep with you all the time in your pocket or purse so that you are ready whenever there may be an opportunity to be a witness.

2. *Go with a partner.* Jesus sent His disciples out in pairs of two: "After these things the Lord appointed other seventy also, and sent them two and two before his face into every city and place, whither he himself would come" (Luke 10:1). There are several reasons why following this precedent is wise.

First, going with a partner allows an experienced soulwinner to train a new soulwinner. This is invaluable. I encourage every experienced soulwinner to periodically ask someone new, "Would you come soulwinning with me? We'll go every week for four or five months, and I'll teach you how to lead someone to Christ." I encourage every inexperienced soulwinner to seek out someone to teach them.

Second, it allows one person to be specifically praying during each conversation. For practical reasons, it's best if only one person leads the conversation and the other avoids inserting himself into the conversation. When I'm with a partner, we often take turns at each house. But the other person agrees to pray.

Third, it allows an extra person to help with distractions that arise. So often, at key moments in a gospel presentation, a child will come in with questions or something else will happen to distract. The non-talking partner at that visit can work to mitigate those distractions—playing or talking with the child, etc.

Fourth, it provides accountability. If someone is counting on you to go soulwinning with them at a pre-scheduled time, it's less easy to decide at the last minute you don't feel like going. Having a partner is like having a pre-arranged encourager—and being that encourager for someone else as well.

Finally, it protects your testimony. There will be occasions when you are making a visit and someone of the opposite sex invites you in. If you don't have a partner with you, you shouldn't go in, but having one allows you to make the visit while still protecting your testimony.

3. Always be polite, courteous, and thoughtful to others. Remember, you were not invited to the person's doorstep. So be polite if they are busy or uninterested. Never be forceful or overbearing. You might have caught them at an off moment, but by being courteous and thoughtful, they are more likely to respond the next time someone from your church goes to their home or witnesses to them in the community.

4. Never criticize another person's beliefs. Consider Jesus' conversation with the woman at the well in John 4. When she tried to lead it into a conflict of beliefs, Jesus brought her back to matters of the heart: "But the hour cometh, and now is, when the true worshippers shall worship the Father in spirit and in truth: for the Father seeketh such to worship him" (John 4:23).

Don't be rude or verbally combative, no matter what is said to you or how you are treated. Remember Proverbs 15:1, "A soft answer turneth away wrath: but grievous words stir up anger." You are not there to argue but to share the gospel. Don't allow yourself to get drawn into an argument. A person may have legitimate questions, but criticizing another church or beliefs will not lead to a productive gospel conversation.

5. Never talk alone with a person of the opposite sex in the house. Romans 14:16 tells us, "Let not then your good be evil spoken of." So avoid a situation that could compromise your testimony.

6. Never talk to a young child without a parent present.
You don't want to catch a parent off guard when they come around from the back yard and see you with an open Bible talking to their nine-year-old. They don't know who you are or what you are teaching their child. Keep any conversation with a young child (when the parent is not present) limited to, "Hey there, is your mom or dad home?"

7. Always seek to be led by the Holy Spirit, to be a good ambassador for Christ, and to be a good representative of your church. There will be many situations that come up which you are not exactly sure how to handle. The best way to respond is to rely on the Holy Spirit's guidance and remember that you are representing both Christ and your church. Philippians 1:27 says, "Only let your conversation be as it becometh the gospel of Christ…." Although this verse is speaking in a larger sense of your entire lifestyle being such as adorns the gospel, it applies here to a specific moment in your lifestyle as well. Always endeavor to respond to situations in a way that is becoming of the gospel you are sharing.

PART THREE

Establishing New Christians

I remember the proud moment of holding each of our four children for the first time. There's something about holding a new baby that brings such joy. As you look at that tiny infant, you realize how vulnerable they are. You feel the weight of responsibility as you realize that they depend on you to be cared for and protected, nurtured, and sheltered.

The same is true of a new Christian. The moment a person trusts Christ as their Saviour, they are born again—a newborn babe in Christ. As a child of God, they receive all the rights and privileges associated with being "in Christ." But just like a new baby, they don't even know what they have been given…or how vulnerable they are.

Satan immediately works to undermine a new Christian's confidence in the gospel, in the promises of God, and in their decision to trust Christ. He tempts them to think that their old life was better and that it is impossible to live for Christ. He sends false teachers to draw them into cult teachings.

What does all of this have to do with soulwinning? Everything. Because the Great Commission does not just instruct us to teach the gospel, but it also instructs us to establish new believers—to encourage them to be baptized and to teach them "all things whatsoever I have commanded you" (Matthew 28:20). When you have the privilege of leading someone to Christ, your investment in their life has only just begun.

We see this so clearly in the Apostle Paul's life. Although Paul was aggressive in his determination to preach the gospel in new cities—places where people had never even heard of

Christ (Romans 15:20)—he was also faithful to go back to those he had led to the Lord and teach them how to live their new lives in Christ. He worked to ground them in their faith and connect them to the local church. He had a passion to see people saved *and* growing in the Lord.

Consider, for instance, when Paul preached in Lystra in Acts 14. There, he led people to Christ, but when unbelieving Jews who hated Paul's message showed up on the scene, they "persuaded the people" to stone Paul and only left him once they believed he was dead.

Hours later, however, Paul got up and, with a broken, aching body, went on to Derbe to preach the gospel. In this, we see Paul's fervency to reach unsaved people with the message of salvation.

But from Derbe, Paul couldn't forget those who had recently been saved in Lystra. So he returned to the very city where he had just been persecuted to follow up on these new converts—to confirm them in the faith. From Lystra, he backtracked further to other cities where he had led people to Christ—Iconium and Antioch.

> *And when they had preached the gospel to that city, and had taught many, they returned again to Lystra, and to Iconium, and Antioch, Confirming the souls of the disciples, and exhorting them to continue in the faith, and that we must through much tribulation enter into the kingdom of God.*—ACTS 14:21–22

Every new Christian needs to be confirmed—that is, to be established. They need someone to care enough to give them spiritual encouragement, support, instruction, and grounding. If we only lead people to Christ, but we do not help strengthen them in the faith, we are not fulfilling all of the Great Commission.

So just how do we confirm people? What does the process of biblical growth look like? Why do new Christians need to be established in their faith?

In the next few chapters, we'll look at how to leave a newly-saved Christian with assurance of salvation, how to lead them in Christian growth, and how to help them come full circle in being able to lead others to Christ.

CHAPTER SEVEN

Early Instruction

Several months ago, I was preaching in San Diego when a man walked up to me after the service. "Pastor Chappell, I don't know if you remember me…." I immediately recognized him—Mike. I had led him to Christ thirty years ago at his home in Northern California.

It was such a joy to see Mike still in church and serving the Lord after all these years. He told me that he serves as a Sunday school teacher in his church, and his grown children are walking with the Lord.

As we talked, he pulled a card out of his wallet with my handwriting on it. It simply had his name with the word "salvation" and the date he trusted Christ. Seeing that card which I had given him so long ago and hearing him tell me "I've kept it in my wallet all these years," brought me back to the day I was sitting in his living room when he prayed to receive Christ as his Saviour.

When I had the privilege of leading Mike to Christ, I did what I've done with so many others—emphasized the promises of God for assurance and encouraged him to begin growing in the Lord. And, as in Mike's life, this kind of early instruction makes a difference for continued growth.

In this chapter, we pick up with the kind of conversations that should take place shortly after someone is saved. Now that you have led someone to Christ, what do they need to know? What can you do to help them grow in their faith? Conversations about these four areas should take place either immediately after salvation or in a follow up visit soon after.

ASSURANCE OF SALVATION

The moment a person is saved, they receive the gift of eternal life. But Satan also begins working to undermine their faith. As mentioned previously, it's not uncommon for a new Christian to experience confusion or doubt early on—sometimes right after the soulwinner leaves, sometimes later.

For this reason, when I lead someone to Christ, I always talk to them for a few minutes about eternal security—the fact that once we become God's child, nothing can change that.

God promises to save all who call on Him for salvation.
Going back to the Scriptures I suggested in Chapter 4 for sharing the gospel, you'll remember that the last verse is Romans 10:13,

"For whosoever shall call upon the name of the Lord shall be saved." So often, when I lead someone to the Lord, I still have my New Testament open to this verse.

After the person prays, I ask them if they did just sincerely call on the Lord from their heart. When they answer that they have, I draw their attention back to Romans 10:13, and I point out that it doesn't say, "Whosoever shall call upon the name of the Lord *might* be saved," but "*shall* be saved." God *promises* to save those who call on Him.

And Titus 1:2 tells us that God "cannot lie." Thus, we have the assurance of His Word that when we call out to Him for salvation, He gives it.

Eternal life is forever.

Additionally, I direct the new Christian's attention back to the end of Romans 6:23: "…but the gift of God is eternal life through Jesus Christ our Lord." I point out that God promised to give them the gift of eternal life—which, by definition, lasts forever. He won't ever take that gift back. It is a gift, and it is eternal.

I also often show them John 10:28–29: "And I give unto them eternal life; and they shall never perish, neither shall any man pluck them out of my hand. My Father, which gave them me, is greater than all; and no man is able to pluck them out of my Father's hand."

Ephesians 1:13 tells us we are "sealed" by the Holy Spirit: "In whom ye also trusted, after that ye heard the word of truth, the gospel of your salvation: in whom also after that ye believed, ye were sealed with that holy Spirit of promise." This is a once-and-for-all, eternally-binding seal.

Being born again makes you part of God's family.

Finally, as I did for Mike, I write the person's name and the date of their salvation on a card that I then leave with them.[1] I explain to them that when they asked Christ to save them, they were "born again," and that today is their spiritual birthday. I do this because I want them to know that this is a date they'll want to remember. Of course, a person doesn't have to remember the date in order to have assurance of their salvation, but doing this helps them understand the significance of their decision.

When we accept Christ, we are born again into the family of God. Once we become a child of God, we remain His child for all of eternity. In John 6:37, Jesus promised, "…him that cometh to me I will in no wise cast out."

One of the ways Satan works to stir doubt in the heart of a new Christian is by bringing accusations to their mind when they sin after they are saved. I try to cut this tactic off by telling them ahead of time that there will be times they sin, but that doesn't make them any less God's child than their own children cease to be theirs because of something they do wrong. I may turn to 1 John 2:1 and explain that when we sin,

---

1.   I used to simply write this on a blank card or a tract. But Striving Together Publications has cards available that list key salvation verses and include a place to write a person's name and date of their salvation.

"we have an advocate with the Father, Jesus Christ the righteous." We talk about the importance of restoring fellowship with the Lord after we sin by confessing the sin to Him and asking for His cleansing.

BAPTISM

Baptism is one of the first steps of obedience for a Christian. It's given in the Great Commission even before the instruction, "Teaching them to observe all things whatsoever I have commanded you…."

When I explain baptism to a new Christian, I'm careful to emphasize that being baptized is in no way part of being saved. It is simply publicly identifying with the Lord and His church.

I often explain baptism on the same visit as when someone gets saved if there is time. If not, I may mention it briefly and then come back within a few days and explain it more thoroughly then. Sometimes, even after I explain it, I leave them with a brochure that gives several Scriptures regarding baptism for them to review. (These brochures are available from Striving Together Publications.)

Baptism is an identification.

The Bible teaches that baptism is a symbol—an outward expression of an inward decision.

One example I like to give is that of a wedding ring. Just as wearing a ring does not make someone married, baptism does not make someone saved. But just as a wedding ring identifies a husband with his wife, baptism identifies a Christian with Christ. That identity is with Christ's death, burial, and resurrection.

> *Know ye not, that so many of us as were baptized into Jesus Christ were baptized into his death? Therefore we are buried with him by baptism into death: that like as Christ was raised up from the dead by the glory of the Father, even so we also should walk in newness of life.*—ROMANS 6:3–4

Baptism also identifies a Christian with the local church and its doctrine. In the New Testament, people who were baptized were added to the church.

> *Then they that gladly received his word were baptized: and the same day there were added unto them about three thousand souls. And they continued stedfastly in the apostles' doctrine and fellowship, and in breaking of bread, and in prayers.*—ACTS 2:41–42

Baptism is for every Christian.

The Bible teaches that baptism is for anyone who has personally accepted Christ as Saviour.

> *And as they went on their way, they came unto a certain water: and the eunuch said, See, here is water; what doth hinder me to be baptized? And Philip said, If thou believest with all thine heart, thou mayest. And he answered and said, I believe that Jesus Christ*

is the Son of God. And he commanded the chariot to stand still: and they went down both into the water, both Philip and the eunuch; and he baptized him.
—ACTS 8:36–38

Baptism should be by immersion.

The word *baptize* literally means "to plunge or to dunk." Because baptism is a picture of Christ's death, burial, and resurrection, only immersion correctly pictures this. We see in the examples in Scripture of people being baptized (such as the one above in Acts 8) that it was always by immersion. Other passages in Scripture that speak of baptism use the word *buried,* showing that baptism in Bible days was understood to be by immersion. (See Romans 6:4 and Colossians 2:12.)

Baptism should take place soon after salvation.

In the Bible, baptism always took place right after salvation. It was an immediate and glad response of someone who was saved and wanted to publicly identify with Jesus.

And they said, Believe on the Lord Jesus Christ, and thou shalt be saved, and thy house. And they spake unto him the word of the Lord, and to all that were in his house. And he took them the same hour of the night, and washed their stripes; and was baptized, he and all his, straightway.—ACTS 16:31–33

Occasionally, a new Christian will mention that they were previously baptized—perhaps sprinkled as an infant or even immersed before their salvation. I go back over the truths above, emphasizing that baptism in Scripture always took place after salvation. If this person has just then prayed to receive Christ as their Saviour, I usually ask, "Now when you were baptized as a baby [or as a child in your grandma's church, etc.], had you understood what we just talked about now, and were you already saved?" That question often helps them see that their previous baptism wasn't a biblical baptism. I then point out that baptism before salvation is simply getting wet. It is not the biblical identification with Christ that baptism was meant to be.

After a new Christian agrees to be baptized, I let them know I'll meet them at church on Sunday. I also take a few minutes to explain the procedure at our church for coming forward at the end of a preaching service during our invitation time. A pastoral staff member or deacon will ask them if they have been saved and then will assist them to our baptism ready areas. (I also let them know that we have baptismal robes, so they don't need to bring a change of clothes.)

When a new Christian is planning to be baptized, especially if they have never been to your church or are new, it's helpful to plan to connect with them at church so you can assist them in knowing when to go forward and can be there to encourage and share that time with them.

Since baptism is meant to be a public identification with Christ, after someone has indicated that they do want to be baptized, I often ask them if they have unsaved family members or friends they could ask to come to church to see them be baptized. This gives them an early opportunity to witness for Christ as they invite their family and friends to a church service where they will hear the gospel.

BIBLE READING AND PRAYER

One of the most exciting things about salvation is that it gives us not *only* a future home in Heaven but also a personal relationship with God—here and now.

A relationship, of course, requires communication, and in our relationship with God, communication takes place through reading the Bible and prayer. Reading the Bible is how we listen to God, and prayer is how we talk to God.

I encourage a young Christian to begin reading their Bible right away—if only a few verses a day. If they don't have a Bible, I buy them one. If they have one already, I show them the table of contents in the front and encourage them to begin reading one of the four Gospels—perhaps Mark or John. I explain that the Gospels describe the life of Christ and are a great way to get to know their Saviour.

CHURCH ATTENDANCE

One final area of great importance in which to encourage a new Christian is church attendance. The local church is an institution that Christ Himself established. He loved the church so much that He gave Himself for it (Ephesians 5:25).

The local church is vital for our spiritual growth and encouragement. It provides not only the teaching and preaching of God's Word, but it provides opportunity to fellowship with brothers and sisters in Christ—your spiritual family. This is why Hebrews 10:25 instructs, "Not forsaking the assembling of ourselves together, as the manner of some is; but exhorting one another: and so much the more, as ye see the day approaching."

When I explain the importance of attending church to someone who just got saved, I point out that just as a new baby needs a family and the love and care that comes with it, so a new Christian *needs* a church. They need the spiritual nourishment of preaching and the spiritual help of a church family.

Attending church can be intimidating for a new Christian. Let them know that you will meet them as they arrive, help them find the nurseries or childcare locations for their children, and sit with them in the service. During their first few services, make a point to introduce them to others who might have something in common with them, to help them develop relationships with their new church family. Over time, their continued faithfulness to church is going to be one of the greatest determining factors of their spiritual growth.

A SOLID STARTING POINT

I don't always share everything in this chapter immediately after someone is saved, and I don't always do it in as much detail as is given here. I definitely leave them with a few verses on eternal security. Sometimes I mention the others in just a few sentences, but all four of these areas are necessary components to growth in the life of a young Christian, and I want to do everything I can to give him a solid start in his Christian life.

In addition to the verses I leave with a new Christian, I always make sure that he has my phone number (and that I have his), and I encourage him to text or call any time with any questions. From there, I pray for him regularly and look toward encouraging long-term growth in his life.

CHAPTER EIGHT

Nurturing Growth

We were seated at the study table in my office, and he, this elected official whom I had been praying for and sharing the gospel with for several years, was giving me a transparent glimpse into the current struggles of his heart.

I shared with him that God offers us a complete change of heart when we receive His Son, and I once again shared the gospel with him—this time, in an almost-hour long conversation, to a receptive heart. This time, he trusted Christ as his Saviour.

A few mornings later, I awoke early with him on my mind. I pulled out my phone, and I texted him a few words of encouragement and 2 Corinthians 5:17, "Therefore if any man be in Christ, he is a new creature: old things are passed away; behold, all things are become new."

His response was immediate: "My wife and I were just laying here in bed reading the Bible. We just read that exact verse."

There is nothing more rewarding than to come alongside a new Christian and help ground him in God's Word, encourage his faith, and guide him in new patterns of Christian living.

There is nothing more needed for that young Christian either. Spiritual maturity, like physical maturity, doesn't take place overnight. Neither does it take place the moment a person is baptized or attends three church services in a row. It takes long-term commitment from spiritual leaders to help someone grow in their faith.

Consider Paul's words to the Christians he had led to Christ at Thessalonica:

> *But we were gentle among you, even as a nurse cherisheth her children: So being affectionately desirous of you, we were willing to have imparted unto you, not the gospel of God only, but also our own souls, because ye were dear unto us. For ye remember, brethren, our labour and travail: for labouring night and day, because we would not be chargeable unto any of you, we preached unto you the gospel of God. Ye are witnesses, and God also, how holily and justly and unblameably we behaved ourselves among you that believe: As ye know how we exhorted and comforted and charged every one of you, as a father doth his children, That ye would walk worthy of*

God, who hath called you unto his kingdom and glory.—1 THESSALONIANS 2:7–12

Young Christians need this kind of atmosphere of acceptance, encouragement, and growth. In this chapter, let's look at a few ways you can nurture that growth in the people you lead to Christ.

FELLOWSHIP AND HOSPITALITY

The local church is to be so much more than just a place where people come, listen to music and a sermon, and leave. It is to be a place where believers encourage one another in spiritual growth. This is why the same verse that commands us not to "forsake the assembling of ourselves together," also says, "but exhorting one another...."

> *Not forsaking the assembling of ourselves together, as the manner of some is; but exhorting one another: and so much the more, as ye see the day approaching.*
> —HEBREWS 10:25

In other words, encouraging one another in Christian growth is to be part of what it means to assemble together. And there is no better time to build these relationships than immediately after someone is saved.

In many churches, the best opportunities for this depth of a spiritually-encouraging relationship take place through adult Bible classes or small groups. But even then, it only happens when Christians are intentional about reaching out to those who are new in the Lord to befriend and encourage them. Most Christians find it easy to be friendly to a guest in their adult Bible class. But a new Christian doesn't just need you to be friend*ly;* they need you to be a *friend.* More than a pat on the back and a glad-you're-here handshake, they need someone to come alongside them in Christian friendship.

Another way to encourage new Christians is through opening your home. When my wife and I have new Christians over to our home, we often invite others who have been saved for a while as well—thus, helping the new believers begin to build other Christian friendships.

Hospitality is all throughout the New Testament, and I believe it was extremely helpful in establishing the first-century Christians in the faith. From Acts 2:42 where the new converts "continued stedfastly in the apostles' doctrine and fellowship," to the qualifications of a pastor including that he be "given to hospitality" (1 Timothy 3:2), to the direct instructions to all Christians to also be "given to hospitality" (Romans 12:32) and "Use hospitality one to another" (1 Peter 4:9)—hospitality is both encouraged and commanded.

So encourage that new Christian by befriending them, inviting them to your home, and introducing them to others as well—especially your pastor, small group leader, and those who can provide specific spiritual instruction and encouragement in their life.

CHURCH INVOLVEMENT

One of the most important truths to remember for a soulwinner who is encouraging a new convert is the importance of the local church in the life of every believer. A soulwinner should beware of being the only point of spiritual influence in a young Christian's life. Although your friendship and care is vital, they *need* a local church as well. They need a pastor, Bible preaching, small group or class accountability, and a church *family*.

Encourage them to be faithful to regularly-scheduled services. Help them enroll in an adult Bible class or small group with others in a similar life stage. Introduce them to your pastor and to others in the church family.

As they begin to grow, encourage them to begin serving others. A very new Christian shouldn't be asked to serve as a Sunday school teacher or in a leadership capacity. But they can jump in with you in many other areas. Invite them to come with you as you minister to shut-ins in the nursing home, stuff bulletins for Sunday, visit students in your Sunday school class, make refreshments for your small group fellowship, volunteer to clean the nurseries…anything that will encourage them to serve others and give them a "place" in the family.

DISCIPLESHIP

Biblically speaking, a *disciple* is a committed follower of Christ, and *discipleship* is a life-long process of growth. John 8:31

records, "Then said Jesus to those Jews which believed on him, If ye continue in my word, then are ye my disciples indeed."

But practically speaking, a structured discipleship meeting can be immensely beneficial in getting this process jump started. Having a weekly discipleship program where a new Christian meets one-on-one with a seasoned Christian for structured instruction while having opportunities to ask questions and, in the process, develop a mentor-type relationship has been very helpful to new Christians in our church. We enroll new Christians in discipleship through the adult Bible class. This allows the class leaders to match a new Christian with a trained discipler from their class and to stay involved in helping nurture growth.[1]

But even that is only part of the picture. Discipleship is more than a weekly meeting; it is a process of spiritual maturity that is produced through hearing preaching, developing a devotional life, being in a Sunday school or adult Bible class, and growing relationships in the local church. Be there to encourage a new Christian in this kind of growth.

Any investment that you make in the life of a young Christian, is a worthwhile investment. And, as you'll discover, it not only encourages their growth, but it encourages your spirit! As John wrote in 3 John 4, "I have no greater joy than to hear that my children walk in truth."

---

1.   For more information on starting and conducting a local church discipleship program, see *Order in the Church* (Striving Together Publications, 2015), Chapter 3.

CHAPTER NINE

Committed to Multiplication

If there is one thing that is clear in the New Testament, it is that the gospel doesn't end with receiving it. It is a truth to pass on to others.

From the woman at the well who immediately "left her waterpot, and went her way into the city, and saith to the men, Come, see a man, which told me all things that ever I did: is not this the Christ?" (John 4:28–29) to the Thessalonicans who told everyone they came in contact with about Christ— "For from you sounded out the word of the Lord not only in Macedonia and Achaia, but also in every place your faith to God-ward is spread abroad; so that we need not to speak any thing" (1 Thessalonians 1:8)—it's clear that *spreading* the gospel is the normal response to *receiving* the gospel.

Our responsibility does not end with leading a person to Christ and seeing them baptized and on their way in spiritual growth. We are to teach them to likewise share the gospel and lead others to Christ.

In other words, God's plan for the spreading of the gospel isn't merely *addition;* it is *multiplication.* When you share the gospel with another person and they trust Christ as their Saviour, that is addition—someone has been added to God's family. But when you then teach that new Christian how to share their faith with others, and now you are *both* sharing the gospel and leading people to Christ, that is multiplication.

This is how the early church grew so quickly in the first century. We see the progression from addition to multiplication in the book of Acts.

First, people were *added* to the church.

Then they that gladly received his word were baptized: and the same day there were added unto them about three thousand souls.—Acts 2:41

Praising God, and having favour with all the people. And the Lord added to the church daily such as should be saved.—Acts 2:47

And believers were the more added to the Lord, multitudes both of men and women.)—Acts 5:14

Then, as these new believers became grounded in God's Word through the instruction of the local church, they *multiplied.*

And in those days, when the number of the disciples was multiplied…—Acts 6:1

And the word of God increased; and the number of the disciples multiplied in Jerusalem greatly; and a great company of the priests were obedient to the faith. —Acts 6:7

Then had the churches rest throughout all Judaea and Galilee and Samaria, and were edified; and walking in the fear of the Lord, and in the comfort of the Holy Ghost, were multiplied.—Acts 9:31

As a soulwinner, you want to be reaching people regularly for Christ and seeing them added to the church. Through the preaching, teaching, and discipleship ministries of a local church, new Christians learn to share their faith, and the process multiplies.

But how can you as an individual Christian participate in this process? How can you be a part of helping young Christians lead others to Christ? In this chapter, we'll look at three ways you can help turn addition into multiplication.

INTENTIONAL INVOLVEMENT

A new Christian has a natural desire for others to hear the gospel. A wise soulwinner will involve a new Christian in sharing his faith and in learning how to do it effectively. There are three very good ways to do this:

Encourage a new Christian to invite others to church.
Even before a young Christian feels ready to personally lead
someone to Christ, they can invite their friends to church
where they will hear the gospel.

Invite a new Christian to go soulwinning with you. One
of the best ways to engage a new Christian in soulwinning is
to simply ask them to go out with you. (Or, if you are already
committed, ask another seasoned soulwinner to take them
out.) Let them watch and learn as you engage people in gospel
conversations. In many ways, soulwinning is better caught
than taught. You can teach someone a gospel presentation with
specific verses, but what they learn from actually going with
you allows them to capture something more than a memorized
plan. They will learn from you to have a burden for lost souls,
to be sensitive to the Holy Spirit as you present the gospel, and
to be a good representative for Christ and His church.

***Offer to help a new Christian share the gospel with
friends and relatives.*** Every new Christian has unsaved friends.
And every new Christian desires for these people to be saved.
When you lead someone to Christ, ask them about their friends,
and offer to help them witness to their friends. This may be by
making a visit together, or it may be by coaching them through
how they can share their testimony with their friends.

PRIVATE PRAYER

Sometimes we pray more fervently for people to *be* saved than
we pray for them after they *are* saved. This should not be. All

throughout Paul's epistles, we see him telling those he had led to Christ that he still prayed for them.

Cease not to give thanks for you, making mention of you in my prayers;—EPHESIANS 1:16

Always in every prayer of mine for you all making request with joy,—PHILIPPIANS 1:4

We give thanks to God and the Father of our Lord Jesus Christ, praying always for you,—COLOSSIANS 1:3

We give thanks to God always for you all, making mention of you in our prayers;—1 THESSALONIANS 1:2

I thank my God, making mention of thee always in my prayers,—PHILEMON 4

Speaking of prayer for new converts, missionary J.O. Fraser said, "Just as a plant may die for lack of watering, so may a genuine work of God die and rot for lack of prayer." If you want to see the person you led to the Lord continue growing in grace and become fruitful in their witness, don't neglect to pray for them.

FAITHFUL TESTIMONY

Finally, if you want to see the gospel multiply, remain faithful yourself. The greatest gift you can give a new Christian is a good example. And one of the most discouraging things for a new Christian is when the person who led them to Christ ceases to be faithful—to the Lord or in sharing the gospel.

Remain faithful as a Christian. Make it your goal that, like the Apostle Paul, you will be able to finish your life still faithful to the Lord and looking forward to meeting Him face to face.

> *For I am now ready to be offered, and the time of my departure is at hand. I have fought a good fight, I have finished my course, I have kept the faith: Henceforth there is laid up for me a crown of righteousness, which the Lord, the righteous judge, shall give me at that day: and not to me only, but unto all them also that love his appearing.*—2 TIMOTHY 4:6–8

Remember that those who you lead to Christ tend to look to you. Make sure then that you are living in a way that points them to Christ. Is your church attendance, devotional life, ministry involvement, family life, relational investments, and daily living something that would encourage a new Christian to continue growing in grace? No one is perfect, but we can be faithful and we can work to have a consistent Christian testimony.

Remain faithful as a soulwinner. The person who taught me how to lead people to Christ was my mother. When I was still in elementary school, she would bring me with her every Saturday as she would go from house to house sharing the gospel.

Today, my mom has Alzheimer's and is losing memories that are important to her. She forgets names and even people.

She can't remember dates or how to do basic activities she used to enjoy.

But there is one thing my mom hasn't forgotten—the gospel.

Just recently, I was with her in a hospital waiting room as my dad was having surgery. In the three or four hours we were there, my mom witnessed to several people and led one to Christ. To hear her share the sweet story of salvation—when she can't remember her address or phone number or even her birthday—brought tears to my eyes.

The next day, we were back in the waiting room as my dad had a follow up procedure. The young man whom my mom had led to Christ the previous afternoon came in as well. Not recognizing him, Mom walked over and once again asked him, "Do you know for sure you are going to Heaven?" She didn't remember him or having shared the gospel with him the day before, but he remembered her and having been saved.

Once again, tears came to my eyes. Here was the person who taught me how to share the gospel almost fifty years ago… still sharing it.

Could I encourage you? Make it your goal that those you lead to Christ will see you continuing to be faithful as a soulwinner through the years—whether it's the following afternoon or the following decade, they will see you continuing to seek out those who are lost and tell them that Jesus saves.

PART FOUR

Being an Effective Witness

If you've ever planted a garden, you know that gardening is a skill of many shades. It requires knowledge, patience, attentiveness, and diligence. And, of course, it also requires the sunshine and rain that only God can provide.

Soulwinning is like gardening in many ways. As we plant the seed of the gospel, we are ultimately dependent on the Holy Spirit to bring a harvest. But there are also skills that we can develop that do influence whether or not we will see a harvest.

For just as if a gardener never plants seeds, he will never gather a harvest, and so if we never share the gospel, we won't ever personally lead others to Christ.

Similarly, just as a gardener develops knowledge and skill regarding when to plant, what to plant, and how to nurture freshly-planted seeds, so a soulwinner can develop in learning how to share the gospel and communicate with people in ways that yield the greatest fruit.

Almost anyone can clear a plot of land, plant some seeds, and see some harvest. But a gardener who studies how to best cultivate the soil and what time of year to plant which seeds and which fertilizer to use for what plants and when to water…will generally produce a fuller harvest.

Even so, some soulwinners become more effective than others, in part because they invest more effort in developing as a soulwinner. They continue to grow in their communication skills, and they study Scripture to be able to answer questions. They learn how to take advantage of opportunities to present the gospel even when they are unexpected, and they are careful to follow up on people who have expressed some interest.

Although we are completely dependent on the power of the Holy Spirit, just as a gardener is completely dependent on the elements of nature, there are ways that we can become more fruitful in our witness.

In this section, we'll look at how we can increase the effect of our efforts for the gospel.

CHAPTER TEN

Using a Prospect List

Our job as soulwinners is to sow the gospel seed—faithfully and regularly. Some people will trust Christ the very first time you share the gospel with them—even if it is the first time they meet you.

But not everyone is saved the first time the seed is sown in his heart. In 1 Corinthians 3:6, the Apostle Paul wrote, "I have planted, Apollos watered; but God gave the increase." Jesus told His disciples in John 4:38, "I sent you to reap that whereon ye bestowed no labour: other men laboured, and ye are entered into their labours."

The soil of many hearts requires cultivating to produce a harvest. Sometimes it takes going back a second and third… and twelfth time before someone trusts Christ as their Saviour.

Sometimes it takes multiple times of planting the gospel, watering through prayer, and going back again and again nurturing a relationship with the goal of a spiritual harvest.

The best way I know how to remain diligent in these types of efforts is to use what I call a "prospect list."

Recently during an Easter service at our church, I noticed a couple who were first-time guests sitting on the front row, attentively listening to every word of the message, although they did not respond to the gospel invitation at the end.

I met them after the service but did not sense it was the right timing to ask them if they were saved. I added them to my prayer and prospect list for continued follow up and made a few efforts to reach them.

Finally, after some phone tag, we set a time when they were able to come by my office at the church. The wife had a clear salvation testimony, but the husband did not. I asked him, "Would you mind if I showed you from the Bible how you can know Christ as your personal Saviour?"

Over the next forty-five minutes, I was able to thoroughly share the gospel with him. I even pulled out a piece of paper and drew a mountain on each end with a large empty space in the middle. I explained that we are on one mountain and God on the other, but our sin is the separation between us and God. I drew little planks jutting out from our mountain and showed him from Ephesians 2:8–9 that our good works or religious activities can't bridge the gap of our sin. I then drew a cross that spanned from one mountain to the other as

I showed him from Romans 5:8 that Christ died for us. That afternoon, I was able to lead this man to Christ in my office.

This meeting happened, however, because of my prospect list. If I had not continued to reach out to set up an appointment, we may never have had an opportunity to discuss the gospel.

So, what is a prospect list? And how is it used? In this chapter, we'll look at some of the common questions soulwinners have regarding how to use this vital tool.

WHAT IS A PROSPECT LIST?

The prospect list is the single most important and effective soulwinning tool for stewarding gospel contacts.

Keeping and maintaining a prospect list allows you to be intentional and persistent in your efforts to develop a relationship and to share the gospel. This list helps me follow up on people I've met out door knocking as well as seeing new Christians baptized, added to the church, and grounded through discipleship.

The prospect list is not complicated. It is a simple list of names with contact information and a record of attempts you've made to make contact. On the following page is a sample page from *The Prayer and Prospect Book* commonly used among our church family.[1]

---

1.   This small book is available through Striving Together Publications.

(01) PROSPECT

DATE OF FIRST CONTACT: ___ / ___ / ___

NAME

_____

ADDRESS

_____

CITY   ZIP

_____

PHONE

_____

EMAIL

_____

POINT OF CONTACT

_____

INTERESTS/BACKGROUND

_____

COMMENTS

_____

_____

FOLLOW UP RECORD DATES

PHONE									
EMAIL									
TEXT									
VISIT									

WHO DO I INCLUDE ON MY PROSPECT LIST?

Add anyone you believe to be a positive contact for the gospel. This may be a guest whom you met at church but is not saved (or not yet added to the church). It may be a coworker or classmate. It may be a business contact—a vendor or a client. It may be someone you meet while you are canvassing a neighborhood with gospel tracts. It may be another parent you meet at the park when you're there with your children. All of these are contacts to add to your prospect list.

This list helps you keep track of any contact whom you can continue to follow up with for the purpose of sharing the gospel.

As it relates to canvassing and church follow-up visits, I like to approach these with a shepherding mentality. I'll do my best at each house or visit to gain an opportunity to share the gospel, but, as described in Chapter 5, if the person is having dinner or it is a bad time for them to listen, I will ask if I can come back later.

Similarly, if a person is receptive to my visit and perhaps even listens to the gospel but doesn't trust Christ, I want to develop a relationship with that person. It may be easier to knock only on fresh doors every time you go out soulwinning, but in doing so, you'll neglect people whose hearts the Holy Spirit began stirring since your first visit.

Also, if a person does trust Christ as Saviour, I don't want to leave this young Christian with a simple admonition to come to church. I'm going to keep following up on him until he is baptized and added to the church.

In any of these cases, I'll give the contact my phone number and ask for his. I'll also jot down his address. All of this information I'll add to my prospect list.

I'm very slow to remove someone from my prospect list, but there are occasions when they have expressed they are no longer interested or they have moved without giving me new contact information that I will remove a person from my list. Even then, I keep praying for them, and if there is an event or a special Sunday at church that I think they would be interested in, I may attempt to renew contact again.

HOW DO I USE MY PROSPECT LIST?

Once someone is added to your prospect list, what do you do with his information? Over time, you will accumulate many names. What do you do with these?

1. Pray daily. You can visit, call, and write notes, but only God can work in hearts. Use your prospect list as a daily prayer list rather than just a contact list, and it will become ten times more valuable.

2. Contact weekly. I strive to contact each person on my prospect list at least once per week with a visit, note, or phone call/text. In some cases, I will make multiple efforts toward a contact in a given week if I don't actually connect with them on the first try. The key here is to diligently pursue them, not to simply ease my mind that I tried to make an effort.

Be sensitive to the Holy Spirit in your efforts. There may be occasions to back off for a period of time or to send a note instead of making a visit. But whatever you do, don't neglect these contacts.

3. *Update regularly.* Your list is only as good as it is current. Be diligent in recording your weekly contacts, and periodically update your entire list.

USE THE TOOL

I'll be honest with you—using a prospect list requires diligence. It takes time to update your list, and it takes intention and effort to make weekly follow up contacts.

But it is a diligence that I have seen God bless both in my own soulwinning and in many other fruitful soulwinners. In fact, every fruitful soulwinner I know uses some form of a prospect list—whether it be a stack of 3x5 cards, a printed booklet, or a typed list.

If you want to see the kind of soulwinning harvest that comes through carefully tending to the gospel seed, I'd encourage you to begin your own prospect list today.

CHAPTER ELEVEN

Developing an Everywhere Mentality

My wife, Terrie, was saved as a ten-year-old through the outreach efforts of a nearby Baptist church. Her mom was saved within a few years, but her dad refused the gospel for years.

When Terrie and I began dating, I began praying with her for her dad's salvation. I tried to witness to him, but, although he gave me permission to marry his daughter (as he sat polishing his rifle—no joke), he wasn't interested in the gospel.

You had to meet my father-in-law to appreciate Terrie's and my courage to continue witnessing to him. His name was Como Cosmo Bianco, and he had a personality that matched his name. A large Italian man, he had been an alcoholic for as long as Terrie could remember, and evidences of his rough life showed in his tough exterior.

Over the years, I continued to witness to Como whenever I could—which was rare, since he usually cut me off when I started. Terrie and I continued to pray for him, and we looked for every opportunity to show love and build our relationship with him.

Finally, almost ten years after we had been married, I tried again. I still don't understand exactly why, other than the work of the Holy Spirit, but this time, Como listened and placed his faith in Christ. From that day forward, Como was a changed man. He loved the Lord, and he reflected that to his family.

A few years later, Como died during what was supposed to be a relatively basic heart surgery. Just before the surgery, he reminded all of us gathered in his hospital room for prayer that he knew where he was going because he knew the Saviour.

When we received the call that Como had gone to Heaven, I was so thankful that we had continued to pray for and witness to him even though at times we wondered if he would ever be saved.

Perhaps you, too, have a "Como" in your family or among your coworkers—someone who you've witnessed to, but has rejected the gospel. Sometimes it's easy to give up on people like Como. Sometimes it's easier to develop the habit of sharing the gospel weekly with strangers than it is to continue sharing the gospel with a lost family member or friend. And sometimes it's easy, even while sharing the gospel with others at scheduled times, to miss windows of opportunity to present the gospel in an everyday encounter.

Acts 8:4 tells us of the early Christians, "Therefore they that were scattered abroad went every where preaching the word." How do we also develop this "everywhere mentality" when we are ready to share the gospel at all times and are seeing fruit among our friends and family?

Allow me to suggest four ways.

SEE PEOPLE AS SOULS.

Although we believe the Great Commission is worthy of—and even calls for—purposed times and strategic plans for spreading the gospel, there is a danger in using *only* those purposed times and strategic plans for sharing the gospel. In reality, however, we are surrounded by people who need the Lord—some of which are our family, friends, coworkers, and neighbors. We want to lead them to Christ as well, even if not on a Thursday night at 6:30 or a Saturday morning at 10:00.

The Bible tells us that when Jesus "saw the multitudes, he was moved with compassion on them" (Matthew 9:36). We too easily see people and are moved with frustration at the inconveniences they may bring or we are moved by intimidation of what they would say if we spoke up with the truth.

But, as we noted in Chapter 1, every person has an eternal soul, and you and I know the truth of salvation. Remember the eternality of a soul as you encounter people throughout your day or week, and it will help to make you more mindful of developing relationships with people with whom you want to share the gospel.

LOOK FOR OPPORTUNITIES.

We have a tendency to "miss the forest for the trees." But there are people all around us who need the Lord. How can you see and seize these opportunities? By specifically looking for them!

For instance, when you make a specific soulwinning visit, go also to the homes on both sides of the people you originally purposed to visit, invite them to church, and see if there is an openness for you to share the gospel with them.

When you're going through the checkout counter at a store, give the clerk a tract with an invitation to your church.

When a coworker tells you about a difficult situation in his life, offer to pray for him, and then tell him what a difference knowing Christ personally makes in your life.

You would be surprised how many opportunities there are to share the gospel when you are looking for them. First Thessalonians 2:4 says, "But as we were allowed of God to be put in trust with the gospel, even so we speak; not as pleasing men, but God, which trieth our hearts." You and I, too, were "put in trust with the gospel." And we should look for opportunities to share it with those around us.

STEWARD RELATIONSHIPS.

Less than two months after Jesus rose from the dead, the Apostle Peter preached in Jerusalem, and Acts 2:41 records, "the same day there were added unto them about three thousand souls." What an incredible victory for the gospel as Peter preached that day!

But do you remember who led Peter to Christ? It was his brother, Andrew. John 1:41 says of Andrew, "He first findeth his own brother Simon, and saith unto him, We have found the Messias, which is, being interpreted, the Christ." Andrew's faithfulness to witness to his own family played a part in the backstory to Pentecost—even though Andrew himself didn't preach the powerful sermon of Pentecost. When you and I steward the relationships God has given us, who knows the outcomes of that faithfulness?

God has placed specific relationships in your life—family, neighbors, coworkers, friends, and even briefer acquaintances such as your barber or accountant or child's soccer coach. See these relationships as a gift from the Lord, and nurture them for the purpose of sharing the gospel.

You may not share the gospel every time you see that person. For instance, if every time I saw my neighbor outside, I invited him to church and asked him if he is on his way to Heaven, pretty soon, he'd start avoiding me and tuning out everything I say to him. But if I nurture a relationship with him, asking the names of his family members and compliment his lawn and am careful not to be a difficult neighbor myself, I'll have more of an entrance into his life.

Of course, I'm not suggesting that you don't witness to someone the first time you meet them. When we have a new neighbor move in, Terrie makes cookies or banana bread, and we go over to meet and welcome them and often invite them to church in that first visit. But what I am suggesting is that if a particular moment isn't the right time or the person doesn't respond to the gospel the first time you share it with them, continue to nurture that relationship.

There are two specific ways you can do this.

First, pray for that person. Begin praying regularly for the salvation of your unsaved family members and others with whom you have regular contact. God uses prayer to soften people's hearts. And praying for them will also make you more observant of opportunities that do arise to share the gospel.

Second, be careful to maintain a good testimony for the Lord. If your coworkers see you being dishonest in your work or your neighbors hear you always losing your temper, they're not going to be open to what you have to share with them. On the other hand, if your extended family sees you loving them when they mock your faith, or your friends see you standing for Christ when it is unpopular, over time, they will see in your life what you are trying to also share with your words.

This is what Philippians 2:14–15 speaks of when it says, "Do all things without murmurings and disputings: That ye may be blameless and harmless, the sons of God, without rebuke, in the midst of a crooked and perverse nation, among whom ye shine as lights in the world."

Think of it this way: another Christian may have the opportunity of a chance-encounter to *tell* the gospel to them, but you have the opportunity to also *live* the gospel before them. Use that opportunity wisely.

OBEY EVERY PROMPTING OF THE HOLY SPIRIT.

One of my favorite soulwinning stories in the New Testament is that of Philip and the Ethiopian man in Acts 8. As you read these verses, picture yourself in Philip's shoes—first, as the Lord tells you to go to the desert (not where you would expect to find someone and share the gospel with them) and then as He tells you to run and catch up with the royal caravan from Ethiopia:

> *And the angel of the Lord spake unto Philip, saying, Arise, and go toward the south unto the way that goeth down from Jerusalem unto Gaza, which is desert. And he arose and went: and, behold, a man of Ethiopia, an eunuch of great authority under Candace queen of the Ethiopians, who had the charge of all her treasure, and had come to Jerusalem for to worship, Was returning, and sitting in his chariot read Esaias the prophet. Then the Spirit said unto Philip, Go near, and join thyself to this chariot.—*ACTS 8:26–29

I can imagine that Philip could have felt uncomfortable with these instructions. But what Philip didn't know is that God had already been working in the Ethiopian man's heart. In fact, the man was right at that moment reading Isaiah 53 and had questions about it that led to a natural presentation of the gospel.

> *And Philip ran thither to him, and heard him read the prophet Esaias, and said, Understandest thou what thou readest? And he said, How can I, except some man should guide me? And he desired Philip that he would come up and sit with him. The place of the scripture which he read was this, He was led as a sheep to the slaughter; and like a lamb dumb before his shearer, so opened he not his mouth: In his humiliation his judgment was taken away: and who shall declare his generation? for his life is taken from the earth. And the eunuch answered Philip, and said, I pray thee, of whom speaketh the prophet this? of himself, or of some other man? Then Philip opened his mouth, and began at the same scripture, and preached unto him Jesus.*—ACTS 8:30–35

Because Philip obeyed the Holy Spirit, as awkward as it may have felt to do so, this man got saved.

When the Holy Spirit nudges your heart to speak to someone about salvation, don't ignore His prompting. Even though the situation may not feel comfortable to you to speak up in, you have no idea how God is already preparing the hearts around you. But He knows, and He does prompt us to witness for Him at just the right moments.

This is one reason why it is important that we seek to be filled with the Holy Spirit. The Holy Spirit indwells us at the moment of salvation (Ephesians 1:13), but being filled with the Spirit is when we yield to Him and allow Him to control us. Ephesians 5:18 instructs, "And be not drunk with wine, wherein is excess; but be filled with the Spirit" (Ephesians 5:18).

When we are living in surrender to the Holy Spirit in all areas of our lives, we will be more sensitive and obedient to His promptings to witness as well. And we'll have the opportunity to share the gospel and bear fruit in times and places we never expected.

CHAPTER TWELVE

Staying Motivated

Bernard "Kip" Lagat is a world-class runner from Kenya who has set records for the 1500, 3000, and 5000 meter runs. During the 2000 Sydney Olympics, an interviewer asked him how his country was able to produce so many great distance runners—a sport that requires intense motivation.

With clever wit, Lagat told the Kenyan strategy for motivating speed in running. "It's the road signs," he said, "'Beware of Lions.'"

Many of us struggle with staying motivated in the things that matter most. We're great at starting a new project, hobby, skill, or venture. But when obstacles come up or time passes by, we lose interest or the will to continue. That may be fine for some areas in life, but it's not fine for soulwinning.

Going with the gospel isn't meant to be a one-week mission; it's not even a one-year mission. It is our great commission *for life.*

Regardless of how motivated we feel on a given day, there is a world in need of a Saviour. And we have been entrusted with the message of salvation.

So how can we stay motivated over the decades to be faithful in our witness? I would suggest these four motives as truths to regularly reflect on, especially when you find your motivation slipping.

THE LOVE OF CHRIST

Every time we share the message of salvation, we're telling someone that Jesus died for them. But sometimes we forget to reflect on the fact that Jesus died for *us.* He died for *me.* This isn't simply a factual message—Jesus died for the world—that we tell; it is a powerful demonstration of love that should fill our own hearts with gratitude.

The Apostle Paul never got over the fact that Christ had saved him, and this knowledge motivated his continued surrender to live for Christ in proclaiming the gospel.

> *For the love of Christ constraineth us; because we thus judge, that if one died for all, then were all dead: And that he died for all, that they which live should not henceforth live unto themselves, but unto him which died for them, and rose again.*
> —2 CORINTHIANS 5:14–15

When you get a fresh glimpse of God's love, a heart-level desire to live for Him wells up in your life. His love for you and your love for Him are the purest of all motivations.

When you feel your motivation for soulwinning beginning to slip, meditate on Christ's love for you. Read the Gospel accounts of Christ's crucifixion (Matthew 27, Mark 15, Luke 23, and John 19), and then go and tell others with fresh gratefulness in your heart.

REALITY OF ETERNITY

We live in a day of short attention spans and constant interruptions. Urgent demands press for our time, and flashy amusements promise stress relief. If we're not careful, we will live shallow, driven lives racing from one urgent demand to the next with our free moments swallowed up in mindless distractions.

In all of this, we forget the realities of eternity. We forget that the people around us are not merely bodies—they have souls that will live somewhere forever. We forget that there is a real Heaven and a real Hell and that those who do not trust Christ as Saviour will go to Hell.

Take a moment to slowly read these verses, spoken by Jesus Himself:

> There was a certain rich man, which was clothed in purple and fine linen, and fared sumptuously every day: And there was a certain beggar named Lazarus, which was laid at his gate, full of sores, And desiring

to be fed with the crumbs which fell from the rich man's table: moreover the dogs came and licked his sores. And it came to pass, that the beggar died, and was carried by the angels into Abraham's bosom: the rich man also died, and was buried; And in hell he lift up his eyes, being in torments, and seeth Abraham afar off, and Lazarus in his bosom. And he cried and said, Father Abraham, have mercy on me, and send Lazarus, that he may dip the tip of his finger in water, and cool my tongue; for I am tormented in this flame. But Abraham said, Son, remember that thou in thy lifetime receivedst thy good things, and likewise Lazarus evil things: but now he is comforted, and thou art tormented.—LUKE 16:19–25

The word that grips me every time I read this passage is *tormented*. A form of it is used three times in just three verses. Hell is a real place with real torment. Let that reality motivate you to share the gospel with the people you love.

I once heard a preacher suggest reading Luke 16 every day to remind yourself of the importance of witnessing for Christ. It's a good idea. Though unseen, the realities of eternity are compelling—if we will pause to consider them.

COMPASSION FOR THE LOST

The ministry of Jesus was characterized with compassion. Four specific times in the Gospels, the Bible records that Jesus was "moved with compassion." That is, His compassion didn't just evoke sympathy, but it moved Him to action.

Real compassion moves us to passionate action. It will be tangibly expressed. For a soulwinner, compassion will be expressed in two ways—to pray for more laborers in the harvest of souls and to be a faithful laborer ourselves.

> But when he saw the multitudes, he was moved with compassion on them, because they fainted, and were scattered abroad, as sheep having no shepherd. Then saith he unto his disciples, The harvest truly is plenteous, but the labourers are few; Pray ye therefore the Lord of the harvest, that he will send forth labourers into his harvest.—MATTHEW 9:36–38

Where does compassion begin? Look back to the beginning of the verses above. "But when he saw the multitudes...." Compassion begins when we see—really see—people. It's when we see people as God sees them.

Jesus didn't see people as numbers but as souls. The Gospel of Mark records that even as Christ gave His disciples the Great Commission, He reminded them of the eternal needs attached to fulfilling it.

> He that believeth and is baptized shall be saved; but he that believeth not shall be damned.—MARK 16:16

Having the compassion of Christ motivates us to be a faithful witness—not just once a week during a scheduled soulwinning time or not just for a few months during a special outreach emphasis, but at all times for the duration of our lives.

THE JUDGMENT SEAT OF CHRIST

Although remembering the reality of Hell and seeing people through eyes of compassion will motivate us to warn them, there is another eternal reality that motivates us with joy. It is the Judgment Seat of Christ.

One day, we will stand before the Lord, and everything that we have done for Him by His grace will be rewarded.

> *...for we shall all stand before the judgment seat of Christ. For it is written, As I live, saith the Lord, every knee shall bow to me, and every tongue shall confess to God. So then every one of us shall give account of himself to God.*—ROMANS 14:10–12

The Judgment Seat of Christ is not a time of accounting for our sins, for that was settled long ago at Calvary. Works do not save us; only faith in Jesus' shed blood for the atonement of our sins gives us eternal life.

But this is a time when our labor for Christ is awarded. The Greek word used in Romans 14 for *judgment seat* is the word *bema*. I have been to the actual bema seat in Corinth where a judge would award prizes to contestants after the Olympic games.

I look forward to the day when I stand before the Lord, and I desire to hear Him say, "Well done, thou good and faithful servant" (Matthew 25:21).

Whatever reward I am given for serving, I will be able to cast at Jesus' feet in worship, acknowledging that He is worthy. Revelation 4:10 speaks of this future moment:

> *The four and twenty elders fall down before him that sat on the throne, and worship him that liveth for ever and ever, and cast their crowns before the throne, saying, Thou art worthy, O Lord, to receive glory and honour and power: for thou hast created all things, and for thy pleasure they are and were created.*
> —REVELATION 4:10–11

Looking forward to this moment motivates us to invest our time and lives in that which matters for eternity. At the end of life, our greatest joy will be the rewards of our eternal investments. The Apostle Paul looked forward to this day with great anticipation, and he expressed that those he had led to Christ and spiritually nurtured in discipleship were his "joy and crown"—his trophy.

> *For what is our hope, or joy, or crown of rejoicing? Are not even ye in the presence of our Lord Jesus Christ at his coming?*—1 THESSALONIANS 2:19

> *Therefore, my brethren dearly beloved and longed for, my joy and crown, so stand fast in the Lord, my dearly beloved.*—PHILIPPIANS 4:1

What a joy it will be to stand before Christ with the fruit of souls! It will only happen, however, as we let biblical motivations—the love of Christ, reality of eternity, compassion for the lost, and the Judgment Seat of Christ—stir our hearts to faithfully, consistently share the gospel message.

We have only a short window of time on earth to witness for Christ. Jesus Himself said, "I must work the works of him that sent me, while it is day: the night cometh, when no man can work" (John 9:4).

So, as we close this book, allow me to challenge you to take the Great Commission of Christ—go, win, baptize, teach— personally. And by that, I mean to not just be comfortable to know others in your church, share the gospel, or to rest in the fact that you are saved and on your way to Heaven.

There are people all around you who don't know the Lord. There are people who God has allowed you to know who perhaps will not hear the gospel from anyone *but* you. And there are people in your community who you could seek out to share the greatest news in all the world.

So take it personally—take the gospel to others. Invest yourself in nurturing their growth. And look forward to standing before the Lord and hearing Him say, "Well done, thou good and faithful servant."

Make His Great Commission your personal priority.

Resources for Outreach and Discipleship

Over the years, we have developed resources for soulwinning, outreach, and discipleship for use here at Lancaster Baptist Church. As the Lord has blessed these in our efforts, we've made them available to other churches through Striving Together Publications. The following is a list of these resources available at strivingtogether.com:

- **Tracts, outreach cards, and print materials**—From 3.5″ x 5.5″ outreach cards to folded tracts, choose from a wide selection of printed tools to clearly communicate the gospel. Available in English and Spanish, preprinted or personalized, these resources are beautiful, affordable, and effective.

- *Paid in Full* **minibook**—Written directly to an unsaved person, this small book explains salvation simply and engages with the reader conversationally. It is a great tool for soulwinning and makes a wonderful gift for unsaved family and friends, follow-up visits, and first-time guests to church.

- **Baptism brochure**—This full color brochure carefully communicates the scriptural importance of baptism to a new convert. It is a perfect tool to use in a follow-up visit and answers the following questions: What is baptism? Is baptism for me? Why should I be baptized? How should I be baptized? When should I be baptized? What if I'm not baptized? What can I expect?

- **Salvation cards**—The size of a credit card, these high-quality, plastic cards feature a brief recap of the gospel along with Scripture references used to share the gospel. With a line for someone to write their name and the date they were saved, these are helpful to leave with someone who just trusted Christ as a record of their decision and a reminder of the truth of salvation.

- *First Steps for New Christians*—This small paperback is designed to help someone who recently trusted Christ to begin learning the basics of the Christian faith and lifestyle. Perfect to use in altar packets or follow-up visits with new Christians, this is a powerful "pre-discipleship" tool that will help to quickly get a new convert on the path of growth and spiritual stability.

- *Continue* **discipleship book**—Featuring fourteen lessons that cover key Bible doctrines with personal applications, *Continue* is perfect for helping a new Christian become grounded in God's Word. Each lesson includes a straightforward outline with thorough support Scriptures and is written so anyone can easily teach it. Additionally, each week includes daily devotions to encourage the new Christian to develop the habit of getting into God's Word.

- *The Prayer and Prospect Book*—This pocket-sized book provides a convenient way to record contact information for gospel prospects and to track your continued contact efforts.

- *Out of Commission*—Written for every Christian who desires to obey the Great Commission of Christ, this comprehensive volume is motivational and practical, diagnostic and corrective. Whether you are new to evangelism or an experienced soulwinner, *Out of Commission* will challenge and equip you to share your faith and more effectively reach your community for Christ.

APPENDIX B

Teaching Outlines

This book was written around easily-teachable outlines and designed to be adaptable for a training setting. By using each of the four book parts as one lesson, you have four lessons. Use the chapters as your main points and the headings as your sub points. The introductions to each of the parts in the book can serve as your introduction to each lesson. (Some chapters also have a concluding heading that can serve as a conclusion to the point.)

A corresponding student workbook which follows this pattern is available through Striving Together Publications. This workbook also includes the support Scriptures found throughout the text.

LESSON 1: MAKING A DIFFERENCE

I. The Value of One

    A. A soul is eternal.

    B. Heaven and Hell are real.

    C. Jesus is the only way of salvation.

II. To Seek and To Save

    A. Go

    B. Win

    C. Baptize

    D. Teach

III. Owning the Mission

    A. Make a commitment.

    B. Set a plan.

    C. Seek God's help.

    D. Prepare a message.

LESSON 2: PRESENTING THE GOSPEL

I. Sharing the Gospel

    A. Understanding the gospel

        1. *Avoid the extremes.*

        2. *Have a plan.*

    B. Giving a clear presentation

        1. *Understand that God loves you.*

        2. *Realize your condition.*

        3. *Notice God's price for sin.*

    4.   *Believe Christ died for you.*

    5.   *Confess your faith in Christ.*

C. Leading to a decision

D. Preparing to share the gospel

II. Dealing with Common Questions

A. Common objections

    1.   *I have always been a Christian.*

    2.   *I've asked God to forgive me many times.*

    3.   *This is too simple. I need to do something to earn it.*

    4.   *I'm good enough. I'm not a very bad sinner.*

    5.   *Doesn't death end everything? How do we know there is a real Heaven and Hell?*

    6.   *I don't want to give up my lifestyle or my friends.*

    7.   *I think as long as I'm sincere in what I believe, that's all that matters.*

B. The Deity of Christ

    1.   *His deity is shown through His names.*

    2.   *His deity is shown through His works.*

    3.   *His deity is shown through worship.*

    4.   *His deity is shown through His attributes.*

    5.   *His deity is shown through His resurrection.*

III. Making a Soulwinning Visit

A. Example conversations

    1.   *For a doorknocking or canvassing visit*

        • Introduce yourself.

- Clearly give the name of your church.
- Explain the purpose for your visit.
- Invite them to your church.
- Determine if this is the right time to continue the visit.
- Look for an opportunity to turn the conversation.
- Exchange contact information.

2. *For a specific visit*

B. Practical tips
1. *Carry a New Testament with you.*
2. *Go with a partner.*
3. *Always be polite, courteous, and thoughtful of others.*
4. *Never criticize another person's beliefs.*
5. *Never talk alone with a person of the opposite sex in the house.*
6. *Never talk to a young child without a parent present.*
7. *Always seek to be led by the Holy Spirit, to be a good ambassador for Christ, and to be a good representative of your church.*

LESSON 3: ESTABLISHING NEW CHRISTIANS

I. Early Instruction

A. Assurance of Salvation

    1. *God promises to save all who call on Him for salvation.*

    2. *Eternal life is forever.*

    3. *Being born again makes you part of God's family.*

B. Baptism

    1. *Baptism is an identification.*

    2. *Baptism is for every Christian.*

    3. *Baptism should be by immersion.*

    4. *Baptism should take place soon after salvation.*

C. Bible Reading and Prayer

D. Church Attendance

II. Nurturing Growth

A. Fellowship and Hospitality

B. Church Involvement

C. Discipleship

III. Committed to Multiplication

A. Intentional Involvement

    1. *Encourage a new Christian to invite others to church.*

    2. *Invite a new Christian to go soulwinning with you.*

    3. *Offer to help a new Christian share the gospel with friends and relatives.*

B. Private Prayer

C. Faithful Testimony

1. *Remain faithful as a Christian.*

2. *Remain faithful as a soulwinner.*

LESSON 4: BEING AN EFFECTIVE WITNESS

I. Using a Prospect List

A. What Is a Prospect List?

B. Who Do I Include on My Prospect List?

C. How Do I Use My Prospect List?

1. *Pray daily.*

2. *Contact weekly.*

3. *Update regularly.*

II. Developing an Everywhere Mentality

A. See People as Souls.

B. Look for Opportunities.

C. Steward Relationships.

D. Obey Every Prompting of the Holy Spirit.

III. Staying Motivated

A. The Love of Christ

B. Reality of Eternity

C. Compassion for the Lost

D. The Judgment Seat of Christ

ACKNOWLEDGMENTS

This book represents the investments of many people, and I am grateful for their contributions.

First, I would like to thank Lancaster Baptist Church for owning and obeying the Great Commission as a church. I thank God for what He has done through you in impacting our valley for Christ over the past thirty years. I believe the best is yet to come, and I'm grateful to labor with you in reaching yet more souls with the gospel.

Also, I'm grateful for the efforts of our ministry staff who have served with me in personal soulwinning and discipleship as they help me to equip our church family for the work of the ministry. Thank you for your labor as unto the Lord.

Finally, I want to thank the team of laborers and volunteers in Striving Together Publications. Thank you for your efforts in bringing this manuscript to completion and your work in making it available to influence others to embrace the Great Commission of Christ.

About the Author

PAUL CHAPPELL is the senior pastor of Lancaster Baptist Church and president of West Coast Baptist College in Lancaster, California. His biblical vision has led the church to become one of the most dynamic Baptist churches in the nation. His preaching is heard on Daily in the Word, a daily radio broadcast heard across America. He has been married to his wife Terrie for thirty-five years, and they have four married children and eight grandchildren. His children are all serving the Lord in full-time Christian ministry.

You can connect with Dr. Chappell through his blog, Twitter, and Facebook:

paulchappell.com
twitter.com/paulchappell
facebook.com/pastor.paul.chappell

Visit us online

strivingtogether.com

wcbc.edu

Also available from
Striving Together Publications

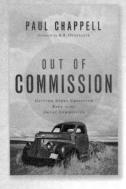

Out of Commission

Written for every Christian who desires to obey the Great Commission of Christ, this comprehensive volume is motivational and practical, diagnostic and corrective. Whether you are new to evangelism or an experienced soulwinner, *Out of Commission* will challenge and equip you to share your faith and more effectively reach your community for Christ. (256 pages, hardback)

Stewarding Life

This book will take you on a personal stewardship journey, equipping you to live effectively and biblically. It will challenge and equip you to strategically invest your most valuable resources for God's eternal purposes. Through these pages, discover God's most important principles for managing His most valuable gifts. (280 pages, hardback)

Living Beyond Your Capacity

The wonderful Holy Spirit of God desires to come into your life at salvation and unfold a daily work of power, grace, and transformation. He can enable you to live a supernatural life—a life that exceeds your human capacity. You can begin discovering and experiencing the Spirit-filled life today! (208 pages, paperback)

strivingtogether.com

Also available from
Striving Together Publications

Stewarding Life
Sunday School Curriculum
Stewarding life begins with a recognition that life itself is a gift from God and that He has provided every resource we need to carry out His purposes. In this thirteen-lesson series, you will discover God's most important principles for managing His most valuable gifts.

Abiding in Christ
Sunday School Curriculum
This unique study of John 15 takes you on a journey of learning how to become more like Christ by abiding in Him on a daily basis.

Real Church
Sunday School Curriculum
In this thirteen-lesson curriculum, discover authentic church life from the dynamic first century churches in the New Testament. Discover how you fit into God's eternal plan for changing the world through your local church.

strivingtogether.com